C

KENTUCKY BIRDS

Michael Roedel
Gregory Kennedy

LONE
PINE

Lone Pine Publishing International

© 2005 by Lone Pine Publishing International Inc.
First printed in 2005   10 9 8 7 6 5 4 3 2 1
Printed in China

The Distributor: Lone Pine Publishing
1808 B Street NW, Suite 140
Auburn, WA, USA 98001

Website: www.lonepinepublishing.com

Library and Archives Canada Cataloguing in Publication

Roedel, Michael, 1955-
   Compact guide to Kentucky birds / Michael Roedel, Gregory Kennedy.

Includes bibliographical references and index.
ISBN-13: 978-976-8200-01-3
ISBN-10: 976-8200-01-4

1. Birds--Kentucky--Identification. 2. Bird watching--Kentucky. I. Kennedy, Gregory, 1956- II. Title.

QL684.K4R63 2006   598'.09769   C2005-907613-5

Cover Illustration: Kentucky Warbler by Ted Nordhagen
Illustrations: Gary Ross, Ted Nordhagen, Eva Pluciennik
Separations & Film: Elite Lithographers Co.

PC: 13

Contents

4 Reference Guide

Canada Goose
size 42 in • p. 18

Wood Duck
size 17 in • p. 20

Mallard
size 24 in • p. 22

Blue-winged Teal
size 14 in • p. 24

Northern Pintail
size 23 in • p. 26

Bufflehead
size 14 in • p. 28

Ruffed Grouse
size 17 in • p. 30

Wild Turkey
size 40 in • p. 32

Northern Bobwhite
size 10 in • p. 34

Pied-billed Grebe
size 13 in • p. 36

Great Blue Heron
size 52 in • p. 38

Green Heron
size 18 in • p. 40

Black-crowned Night-Heron
size 25 in • p. 42

Turkey Vulture
size 28 in • p. 44

Bald Eagle
size 36 in • p. 46

Broad-winged Hawk
size 16 in • p. 48

Red-tailed Hawk
size 21 in • p. 50

American Kestrel
size 8 in • p. 52

COOTS & CRANES

American Coot
size 14 in • p. 54

Sandhill Crane
size 45 in • p. 56

Killdeer
size 10 in • p. 58

SHOREBIRDS

Lesser Yellowlegs
size 10 in • p. 60

Spotted Sandpiper
size 7 in • p. 62

Ring-billed Gull
size 19 in • p. 64

GULLS

Rock Pigeon
size 12 in • p. 66

Mourning Dove
size 12 in • p. 68

Yellow-billed Cuckoo
size 12 in • p. 70

DOVES & CUCKOOS

Eastern Screech-Owl
size 8 in • p. 72

Great Horned Owl
size 22 in • p. 74

Common Nighthawk
size 9 in • p. 76

OWLS

Whip-poor-will
size 9 in • p. 78

Chimney Swift
size 5 in • p. 80

Ruby-throated Hummingbird
size 4 in • p. 82

NIGHTJARS & HUMMINGBIRDS

Belted Kingfisher
size 12 in • p. 84

Red-headed Woodpecker
size 9 in • p. 86

Red-bellied Woodpecker
size 10 in • p. 88

WOODPECKERS

WOODPECKERS

Downy Woodpecker
size 6 in • p. 90

Northern Flicker
size 12 in • p. 92

Pileated Woodpecker
size 16 in • p. 94

FLYCATCHERS

Eastern Wood-Pewee
size 6 in • p. 96

Acadian Flycatcher
size 6 in • p. 98

Eastern Phoebe
size 7 in • p. 100

SHRIKES & VIREOS

Great Crested Flycatcher
size 8 in • p. 102

Eastern Kingbird
size 9 in • p. 104

Loggerhead Shrike
size 9 in • p. 106

JAYS & CROWS

White-eyed Vireo
size 5 in • p. 108

Blue Jay
size 11 in • p. 110

American Crow
size 18 in • p. 112

SWALLOWS

Purple Martin
size 8 in • p. 114

Northern Rough-winged Swallow
size 6 in • p. 116

Barn Swallow
size 7 in • p. 118

CHICKADEES, NUTHATCHES & WRENS

Carolina Chickadee
size 4 in • p. 120

Tufted Titmouse
size 6 in • p. 122

White-breasted Nuthatch
size 6 in • p. 124

WRENS

THRUSHES

MIMICS, STARLINGS & WAXWINGS

WOOD-WARBLERS & TANAGERS

SPARROWS, GROSBEAKS & BUNTINGS

Carolina Wren
size 5 in • p. 126

Eastern Bluebird
size 7 in • p. 128

Wood Thrush
size 8 in • p. 130

American Robin
size 10 in • p. 132

Gray Catbird
size 9 in • p. 134

Northern Mockingbird
size 10 in • p. 136

Brown Thrasher
size 11 in • p. 138

European Starling
size 8 in • p. 140

Cedar Waxwing
size 7 in • p. 142

Ovenbird
size 6 in • p. 144

Common Yellowthroat
size 5 in • p. 146

Kentucky Warbler
size 5 in • p. 148

Yellow-breasted Chat
size 7 in • p. 150

Scarlet Tanager
size 7 in • p. 152

Eastern Towhee
size 8 in • p. 154

Field Sparrow
size 6 in • p. 156

White-throated Sparrow
size 7 in • p. 158

Dark-eyed Junco
size 6 in • p. 160

Northern Cardinal
size 8 in • p. 162

Blue Grosbeak
size 7 in • p. 164

Indigo Bunting
size 5 in • p. 166

Red-winged Blackbird
size 8 in • p. 168

Eastern Meadowlark
size 9 in • p. 170

Common Grackle
size 12 in • p. 172

Brown-headed Cowbird
size 7 in • p. 174

Orchard Oriole
size 7 in • p. 176

House Finch
size 5 in • p. 178

American Goldfinch
size 5 in • p. 180

House Sparrow
size 6 in • p. 182

Introduction

If you have ever admired a songbird's pleasant notes, been fascinated by a soaring hawk or wondered how woodpeckers keep sawdust out of their nostrils, this book is for you. There is so much to discover about birds and their surroundings that birding is becoming one of the fastest growing hobbies on the planet. Many people find it relaxing, while others enjoy its outdoor appeal. Some people see it as a way to reconnect with nature, an opportunity to socialize with like-minded people or a way to monitor the environment.

Whether you are just beginning to take an interest in birds or can already identify many species, there is always more to learn. We've highlighted both the remarkable traits and the more typical behaviors displayed by some of our most abundant or noteworthy birds. A few live in specialized habitats, but most are common species that you have a good chance of encountering on most outings or in your backyard.

BIRDING IN THE GRASSLANDS

We are truly blessed by the geographical and biological diversity of Kentucky. In addition to supporting a wide range of breeding birds and year-round residents, our state hosts a large number of spring and fall migrants that move through our area on the way to their breeding and wintering grounds. In all, 369 bird species have been seen and recorded in Kentucky.

Identifying birds in action and under varying conditions involves skill, timing and luck. The more you know about a bird—its range, preferred habitat, food preferences and hours and seasons of activity—the better your

Cedar Waxwing

chances will be of seeing it. Generally, spring and fall are the busiest birding times. Temperatures are moderate then, many species of birds are on the move, and male songbirds are belting out their unique courtship songs. Birds are usually most active in the early morning hours, except in winter, when they forage during the day when milder temperatures prevail.

Another useful clue for correctly recognizing birds is knowledge of their habitat. Simply put, a bird's habitat is the place where it normally lives. Some birds prefer open water, some are found in cattail marshes, others like mature coniferous forest, and still other birds prefer abandoned agricultural fields overgrown with tall grass and shrubs. Habitats are just like neighborhoods: if you associate friends with the suburb in which they live, you can easily learn to associate specific birds with their preferred habitat. Only in migration, especially during inclement weather, do some birds leave their usual habitat.

Recognizing birds by their songs and calls can greatly enhance your birding experience. Numerous tapes and CDs are available to help you learn bird songs, and a portable player with headphones can let you quickly compare a live bird with a recording. The old-fashioned way to remember bird songs is to make up words for them. We have given you some of the classic renderings in the species accounts that follow. Some of these approximations work better than others; birds often add or delete syllables from their calls, and very few pronounce consonants in a recognizable fashion. Remember, too, that songs may vary from place to place.

Bald Eagle

Kentucky has a long tradition of friendly, recreational birding. In general, birders are willing to help beginners, share their knowledge and involve novices in their projects. Christmas bird counts, breeding bird surveys, nest box programs, migration monitoring, and birding lectures and workshops provide a chance for bird-watchers of all levels to interact and share the splendor of birds. Bird hotlines provide up-to-date information on the sightings of rarities, which are often easier to relocate than you might think. For more information or to participate in these projects, contact the following organizations:

Kentucky Ornithological Society
http://www.biology.eku.edu/kos.htm

Audubon in the State of Kentucky
http://www.audubon.org/states/ky/

Kentucky Department of Fish and Wildlife Resources Watchable Wildlife and Birding Trails Guide
http://www.kdfwr.state.ky.us/

BIRD LISTING
Many birders list the species they have seen during excursions or at home. It is up to you to decide what kind of list—systematic or casual—you will keep, and you may choose not to make lists at all. Lists may prove rewarding in unexpected ways, and after you visit a new area, your list becomes a souvenir of your experiences there. It can be interesting to compare the arrival dates and last sightings of hummingbirds and

Barn Swallow

other seasonal visitors, or to note the first sighting of a new visitor to your area.

BIRD FEEDING

Many people set up bird feeders in their backyard, especially in winter. It is possible to attract specific birds by choosing the right kind of food and style of feeder. Keep your feeder stocked through late spring, because birds have a hard time finding food before the flowers bloom, seeds develop and insects hatch. Contrary to popular opinion, birds do not become dependent on feeders, nor do they subsequently forget to forage naturally. Be sure to clean your feeder and the surrounding area regularly to prevent the spread of disease.

Landscaping your property with native plants is another way of providing natural food for birds. Flocks of waxwings have a keen eye for red mountain ash berries and hummingbirds enjoy columbine flowers. The cumulative effects of "nature-scaping" urban yards can be a significant step toward habitat conservation (especially when you consider that habitat is often lost in small amounts—a seismic line is cut in one area and a highway is built in another). Many good books and web sites about attracting wildlife to your backyard are available.

NEST BOXES

Another popular way to attract birds is to put up nest boxes, especially for House Wrens, Eastern Bluebirds, Tree Swallows and Purple Martins. Not all birds will use nest boxes: only species that normally use cavities in trees are comfortable in such confined spaces. Larger nest boxes can attract kestrels, owls and cavity-nesting ducks.

Downy Woodpecker

ABOUT THE SPECIES ACCOUNTS

This book gives detailed accounts of 83 species of birds that can be expected in Kentucky on an annual basis. The order of the birds and their common and scientific names follow the American Ornithologists' Union's *Check-list of North American Birds* (7th edition, July 1998, and its supplements through 2005).

As well as showing the identifying features of the bird, each species account also attempts to bring the bird to life by describing its various character traits. One of the challenges of birding is that many species look different in spring and summer than they do in fall and winter. Many birds have breeding and nonbreeding plumages, and immature birds often look different from their parents. This book does not try to describe

Eastern Bluebird

or illustrate all the different plumages of a species; instead, it tries to focus on the forms that are most likely to be seen in our area.

ID: Large illustrations point out prominent field marks that will help you tell each bird apart. The descriptions favor easily understood language instead of technical terms.

Other ID: This section lists additional identifying features. Some of the most common anatomical features of birds are pointed out in the Glossary illustration (p. 185).

Size: The average length of the bird's body from bill to tail, as well as wingspan, are given and are approximate measurements of the bird as it is seen in nature. The size is sometimes given as a range, because there is variation between individuals, or between males and females.

Voice: You will hear many birds, particularly songbirds, which may remain hidden from view. Memorable paraphrases of distinctive sounds will aid you in identifying a species by ear.

Status: A general comment, such as "common," "uncommon" or "rare," is usually sufficient to describe the relative abundance of a species. Situations are bound to vary somewhat since migratory pulses, seasonal changes and centers of activity tend to concentrate or disperse birds.

Habitat: The habitats listed describe where each species is most commonly found. Because of the freedom that flight gives them, birds can turn up in almost any type of habitat. However, they will usually be found in environments that provide the specific food, water, cover and, in some cases, nesting habitat that they need to survive.

Northern Cardinal

Similar Birds: Easily confused species are illustrated for each account. If you concentrate on the most relevant field marks, the subtle differences between species can be reduced to easily identifiable traits. Even experienced birders can mistake one species for another.

Nesting: In each species account, nest location and structure, clutch size, incubation period and parental duties are discussed. A photo of the bird's egg is also provided. Remember that birding ethics discourage the disturbance of active bird nests. If you disturb a nest, you may drive off the parents during a critical period or expose defenseless young to predators.

Range Maps: The range map for each species shows the overall range of the species in an average year. Most birds will confine their annual movements to this range, although each year some birds wander beyond their traditional boundaries. The maps show breeding, summer and winter ranges, as well as migratory pathways—areas of the region where birds may appear while en route to nesting or winter habitat. The representations of the pathways do not distinguish high-use migration corridors from areas that are seldom used.

Range Map Symbols

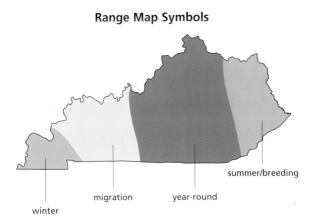

summer/breeding

migration year-round

winter

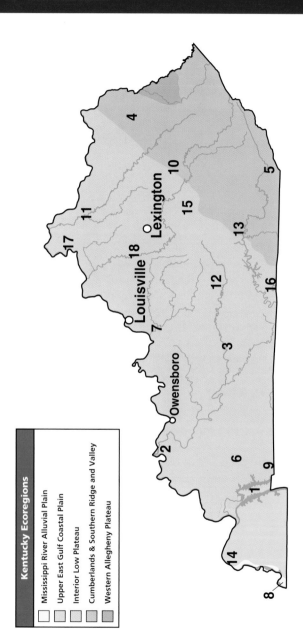

Kentucky Ecoregions

Mississippi River Alluvial Plain
Upper East Gulf Coastal Plain
Interior Low Plateau
Cumberlands & Southern Ridge and Valley
Western Allegheny Plateau

TOP BIRDING SITES

From the lowlands of the Mississippi Floodplain to the uplands of the Western Allegheny Plateau, our state can be separated into five natural regions: the Mississippi River Alluvial Plain, Upper East Gulf Coastal Plain, Interior Low Plateau, Cumberlands and Southern Ridge and Valley, and the Western Allegheny Plateau. Each region is composed of a number of different habitats that support a wealth of wildlife.

There are hundreds of good birding areas throughout our region. The following areas have been selected to represent a broad range of bird communities and habitats, with an emphasis on accessibility.

1. Land Between the Lakes
2. John James Audubon SP
3. Mammoth Cave NP
4. Grayson Lake SP
5. Pine Mountain SP
6. Pennyrile Forest SP
7. Fort Knox
8. Reelfoot Lake
9. Fort Campbell
10. Natural Bridge SP
11. Kinkaid Lake SP
12. Green River Lake WMA
13. Ano Strip Mines
14. Ballard WMA
15. Central Kentucky WMA
16. Dale Hollow Lake WMA
17. Big Bone Lick SP
18. Buckley Wildlife Sanctuary

NP - National Park
SP - State Park
WMA - Wildlife Management Area

Canada Goose
Branta canadensis

Canada Geese mate for life and are devoted parents. Unlike most birds, the family stays together for nearly a year, which increases the survival rate of the young. Rescuers who care for injured geese report that these birds readily adopt their human caregivers. However, wild geese can be aggressive, especially when defending young or competing for food. Hissing sounds and low, outstretched necks are signs that you should give these birds some space. • The Canada Goose was split into two species in 2004. The larger subspecies, including geese that breed in Kentucky and other southern states, are known as Canada Geese, while the smaller, arctic-breeding subspecies have been renamed Cackling Geese.

Other ID: dark brown upperparts; light brown underparts. *In flight:* flocks fly in V-formation.
Size: L 3–4 ft; W up to 6 ft.
Voice: loud, familiar *ah-honk*.
Status: common permanent resident.
Habitat: lakeshores, riverbanks, ponds, farmlands and city parks.

Similar Birds

Cackling Goose

Brant

long, black neck

white "chin strap"

short, black tail

white undertail coverts

Nesting: usually on the ground; female builds a nest of grass and mud, lined with down; white eggs are 3½ x 2¼ in; female incubates 3–8 eggs for 25–28 days; goslings hatch in May.

Did You Know?

Canada Geese have been kept in captivity since the early 1800s, including a flock kept at Henderson by ornithologist John James Audubon.

Look For

Geese graze on aquatic grasses and sprouts, and you can spot them tipping up to grab for aquatic roots and tubers.

Wood Duck

Aix sponsa

As their name implies, Wood Ducks are forest-dwelling ducks, equipped with fairly sharp claws for perching on branches and nesting in tree cavities.
• Female Wood Ducks often return to the same nest site year after year, especially after successfully raising a brood. The young's chance of survival may increase at traditional nest sites, where the adults are familiar with potential threats. If Wood Ducks nest in a local park or farmyard, do not approach the nest, because fewer disturbances·increase the young's chance of survival.

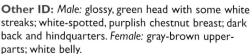

Other ID: *Male:* glossy, green head with some white streaks; white-spotted, purplish chestnut breast; dark back and hindquarters. *Female:* gray-brown upperparts; white belly.
Size: *L* 15–20 in; *W* 30 in.
Voice: *Male:* ascending *ter-wee-wee*. *Female:* squeaky *woo-e-e-k*.
Status: common migrant and summer resident; rare winter resident.
Habitat: swamps, ponds, marshes and lakeshores with wooded edges.

Similar Birds

Hooded Merganser

Look For

Thousands of nest boxes erected across the Wood Duck's breeding range and hunting restrictions have helped Wood Ducks recover from near extinction.

head raised

♂

white, teardrop-shaped eye patch

♀

crest is slicked back from crown

black and white shoulder slash

♀

♂

white "chin" and throat

golden sides

mottled brown breast streaked with white

Nesting: in a hollow, tree cavity or artificial nest box; usually near water; cavity is lined with down; white to buff eggs are 2⅛ x 1⅝ in; female incubates 9–14 eggs for 25–35 days.

Did You Know?

Hatched in a nest cavity that may be 20 feet or more up in a tree, the ducklings must jump to the ground. Like downy ping-pong balls, they bounce on landing and are seldom injured.

Mallard
Anas platyrhynchos

The male Mallard, with his shiny green head and chestnut brown breast, is the classic wild duck. Mallards can be seen year-round, often in flocks and always near open water. • After breeding, male ducks lose their elaborate plumage, helping them stay camouflaged during their flightless period. In early fall, they molt back into breeding colors. • Mallards will freely hybridize with American Black Ducks as well as domestic ducks. The resulting offspring are a confusing blend of both parental types.

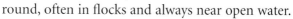

Other ID: orange feet. *Male:* white "necklace"; black tail feathers curl upward. *Female:* mottled brown overall.
Size: *L* 20–28 in; W 3 ft.
Voice: quacks; female is louder than male.
Status: common permanent resident.
Habitat: lakes, wetlands, rivers, city parks, agricultural areas and sewage lagoons.

Similar Birds

Northern Shoveler   American Black Duck   Common Merganser

glossy, green head

yellow bill

dark blue speculum
bordered by white

♂

♀

orange bill
spattered
with black

Nesting: female builds a grass nest on the ground
or under a bush; creamy, grayish or greenish white
eggs are 2¼ x 1⅝ in; female incubates 7–10 eggs
for 26–30 days.

Did You Know?

A nesting hen generates
enough body heat to make
the grasses around her
nest grow faster. She uses
the tall grasses to further
conceal her precious nest.

Look For

These confident ducks can
sometimes be spotted dab-
bling in outdoor swimming
pools.

Blue-winged Teal
Anas discors

Small, speedy Blue-winged Teal are renowned for their aviation skills. They can be identified by their small size and by the sharp twists and turns they execute in flight. • Blue-winged Teal and other dabbling ducks feed by tipping up their tails and dunking their heads underwater. Dabbling ducks have small feet situated near the center of their bodies. Other ducks, such as scaup, scoters and Bufflehead, dive underwater to feed, propelled by large feet set farther back on their bodies.

Other ID: broad, flat bill. *Male:* white undertail coverts. *Female:* mottled brown overall.
Size: L 14–16 in; W 23 in.
Voice: *Male:* soft *keck-keck-keck. Female:* soft quacks.
Status: common migrant; rare summer and winter resident.
Habitat: shallow lake edges and wet-lands; prefers areas with short but dense emergent vegetation.

Similar Birds

Green-winged Teal

Northern Shoveler

green speculum

blue forewing patch

white throat

♀

white crescent on face

blue-gray head

black-spotted breast and sides

♂

Nesting: does not nest in Kentucky; nests in the north-central U.S. and Canada; along a grassy shoreline or in a meadow; nest is built with grass and considerable amounts of down; whitish eggs are 1¾ x 1¼ in; female incubates 8–13 eggs for 23–27 days.

Did You Know?

Blue-winged Teal migrate farther than most ducks, summering as far north as the Canadian tundra and overwintering in Central and South America.

Look For

The male Blue-winged Teal has a white crescent patch next to its bill that is visible year-round.

Northern Pintail
Anas acuta

Its long neck and long, tapered tail put this dabbling duck in a class of its own. The elegant and graceful Northern Pintail breeds in Asia and northern Europe, as well as in North America. • These migrants move through the state early to scout out flooded agricultural fields farther north for choice nesting locations. Unfortunately, Northern Pintails usually build their nests in vulnerable areas, on exposed ground near water, which has resulted in a slow decline in their population.

Other ID: dark, glossy bill. *Male:* dusty gray body plumage; black and white hindquarters. *Female:* mottled, light brown overall.
Size: *Male:* L 25–30 in; W 34 in. *Female:* L 20–22 in; W 34 in.
Voice: *Male:* soft, whistling call.
Female: rough quack.
Status: fairly common migrant; uncommon winter resident.
Habitat: shallow wetlands, flooded fields and lake edges.

Similar Birds

Mallard (p. 22)   Gadwall   Blue-winged Teal (p. 24)

white wing edge

chocolate brown head

white on breast extends up sides of long, slender neck

long, tapering tail feathers

Nesting: does not nest in Kentucky; nests in the north-central U.S., Canada and Alaska; in a small depression in vegetation; nest of grass, leaves and moss is lined with down; greenish buff eggs are $2\frac{1}{8}$ x $1\frac{1}{2}$ in; female incubates 6–12 eggs for 22–25 days.

Did You Know?

In fall, Northern Pintails gather in roosts at marshes and reservoirs, but they fly miles to outlying areas to feed, usually at dusk.

Look For

The long, pointed tail of the male Northern Pintail is easily seen in flight and points skyward when the bird tips up to dabble.

Bufflehead
Bucephala albeola

The typical Bufflehead spends its entire life in
North America, dividing its time between breeding
grounds in the boreal forests of Canada and Alaska
and winter territory primarily in marine bays and
estuaries along the Atlantic and Pacific coasts.
Many of these ducks migrate through Kentucky,
and a few stay on to overwinter on our larger lakes
and rivers. • Fish, crustaceans and mollusks make
up a major portion of the Bufflehead's winter
diet, but in summer this duck eats large
amounts of aquatic invertebrates
and tubers.

Other ID: small, rounded body; short neck. *Male:*
white neck and upperparts; dark back. *Female:* dark
brown head.
Size: *L* 13–15 in; *W* 21 in.
Voice: *Male:* growling call. *Female:* harsh quack.
Status: fairly common migrant; uncom-
mon winter resident.
Habitat: open water on lakes,
large ponds and rivers.

Similar Birds

Hooded Merganser

Common Goldeneye

white speculum ♂

♀

white, oval
ear patch

iridescent, dark green
or purple head

white wedge
on back
of head

short, gray
bill

♀

♂

light brown sides

Nesting: does not nest in Kentucky; nests mainly
in Canada and Alaska; in a tree cavity; often near
water; pale buff to cream-colored eggs are 2 ×
1½ in; female incubates 6–12 eggs for 28–33 days.

Did You Know?

Bufflehead are part of
the "sea duck" group.
These ducks are skilled
divers and can tolerate salt
water and cold climates.

Look For

The white patch on the back
of the male's head stands
out, even at a distance.

Ruffed Grouse
Bonasa umbellus

Should you happen to hear a low "booming" sound echoing through the forest, you are most likely listening to a male Ruffed Grouse "drumming" to announce his territory. Every spring, and occasionally in fall, the male grouse struts along a fallen log with his tail fanned and his neck feathers ruffed, beating the air periodically with accelerating wing strokes. • Ruffed Grouse occur as far north as Alaska. In winter, scales grow out along the sides of the Ruffed Grouse's feet, creating temporary "snowshoes." • Look for this bird in the rugged forests of the Cumberland Mountains.

Other ID: mottled, grayish brown overall. *Female:* incomplete tail band. *Rufous morph:* reddish overall.
Size: L 15–19 in; W 22 in.
Voice: *Male:* hollow, drumming courtship display of accelerating, deep booms. *Female:* clucks and "hisses" around her chicks.
Status: fairly common permanent resident in eastern Kentucky.
Habitat: deciduous and mixed forests and riparian woodlands; favors young, second-growth stands with birch and poplar.

Similar Birds

Northern Bobwhite
(p. 34)

Look For

When a potential threat approaches, a Ruffed Grouse will often freeze to camouflage itself against the forest floor. For every grouse seen, many more go unnoticed.

small, pointed
head crest

black feathers on
sides of lower
neck

barred tail has broad,
dark tail band

dark barring
on sides

rufous morph

Nesting: in a shallow depression among leaf
litter; buff-colored eggs are 1½ x 1⅛ in; female
incubates 9–12 eggs for 23–25 days.

Did You Know?

Ruffed Grouse occur in two morphs, gray and rufous. The
gray morph predominates in the northern parts of the bird's
range; the rufous morph is more common in the south.

Wild Turkey
Meleagris gallopavo

The Wild Turkey was once common throughout most of eastern North America, but in the early 20th century, habitat loss and overhunting took a toll on this bird. Today, efforts at restoration have reestablished the Wild Turkey in many areas of Kentucky. • This charismatic bird is the only native North American animal that has been widely domesticated. The wild ancestors of most domestic animals came from Europe. Early in life both male and female turkeys gobble. The females eventually outgrow this practice, leaving the males to gobble competitively for the honor of mating.

Other ID: dark, glossy, iridescent body plumage; largely unfeathered legs. *Male:* red wattles; black-tipped breast feathers. *Female:* smaller; blue-gray head; less iridescent body; brown-tipped breast feathers.
Size: *Male: L* 3–3½ ft; *W* 5½ ft. *Female: L* 3 ft; *W* 4 ft.
Voice: wide array of sounds; courting male gobbles loudly; alarm call is a loud *pert;* gathering call is a cluck; contact call is a loud *keouk-keouk-keouk.*
Status: common permanent resident.
Habitat: deciduous, mixed and riparian woodlands; occasionally in farm fields in late fall and winter.

Look For

Eastern Wild Turkeys have brown or rusty tail tips and are slimmer than domestic turkeys, which have white tail tips.

naked, blue
red head

barred, copper-colored tail

long central
breast tassel

Nesting: under thick cover in a woodland or at a field edge; in a depression on ground, lined with vegetation; brown-speckled, pale buff eggs are 2½ x 1¾ in; female incubates 10–12 eggs for up to 28 days.

Did You Know?

If Congress had taken Benjamin Franklin's advice in 1782, our national emblem would be the Wild Turkey instead of the majestic Bald Eagle.

Northern Bobwhite
Colinus virginianus

The characteristic, whistled *bob-white* call of our only native quail is heard throughout Kentucky in spring. The male's well-known call is often the only evidence of this bird's presence among the dense, tangled vegetation of its rural, woodland home.
• Throughout fall and winter, Northern Bobwhite typically travel in large family groups called coveys. When a predator approaches, the covey bursts into flight, creating a confusing flurry of activity. With the arrival of summer, breeding pairs break away from their coveys to perform elaborate courtship rituals in preparation for another nesting season.

Other ID: mottled brown, buff and black upperparts; white crescents and spots edged in black on chestnut brown sides and upper breast; short tail.
Size: *L* 10 in; *W* 13 in.
Voice: whistled *hoy* is given year-round. *Male:* a whistled, rising *bob-white* in spring and summer.
Status: fairly common permanent resident.
Habitat: farmlands, open woodlands, woodland edges, grassy fencelines, roadside ditches and brushy, open country.

Similar Birds

Ruffed Grouse (p. 30)

Look For

Bobwhite benefit from habitat disturbance and are often found in the early succession habitats created by fire, agriculture and forestry.

buff throat and "eyebrow"

broad, white "eyebrow"

white throat

rufous breast

♂ ♀

Nesting: in a shallow depression on the ground, often concealed by vegetation or a woven, partial dome; nest is lined with grass and leaves; white to pale buff eggs are 1¼ x 1 in; pair incubates 12–16 eggs for 22–24 days.

Did You Know?

Northern Bobwhite huddle together on cold winter nights, with each bird facing outward, enabling the group to detect danger from any direction.

Pied-billed Grebe
Podilymbus podiceps

Relatively solid bones and the ability to partially deflate its air sac allows the Pied-billed Grebe to sink below the surface of the water like a tiny submarine. The inconspicuous grebe can float low in the water or submerge with only its nostrils and eyes showing above the surface. • While Pied-billed Grebes are year-round residents in Kentucky, they are most common from September to May, when solitary individuals are often seen on larger rivers and lakes.

nonbreeding

Other ID: *Breeding:* white undertail coverts; pale belly. *Nonbreeding:* bill lacks black ring; white "chin" and throat; brownish crown.
Size: L 12–15 in; W 16 in.
Voice: loud, whooping call begins quickly, then slows down: *kuk-kuk-kuk cow cow cow cowp cowp cowp.*
Status: fairly common in migration; rare in winter and summer.
Habitat: ponds, marshes and backwaters with sparse emergent vegetation.

Similar Birds

American Coot (p. 54)

Horned Grebe

dark eye with
pale ring

black ring on
pale bill

all-brown body

very
short tail

breeding

black throat

Nesting: in a wetland; floating platform nest of decaying plants is anchored to emergent vegetation; white to buff eggs are 1⅝ x 1¼ in; pair incubates 4–5 eggs for about 23 days and raises the striped young together.

Did You Know?

When frightened by an intruder, these grebes cover their eggs and slide underwater, leaving a nest that looks like nothing more than a mat of debris.

Look For

Dark plumage, individually webbed toes and a chickenlike bill distinguish Pied-billed Grebes from other waterfowl.

Great Blue Heron
Ardea herodias

The long-legged Great Blue Heron has a stealthy, often motionless hunting strategy. It waits for a fish or frog to approach, spears the prey with its bill, then flips its catch into the air and swallows the prey whole. Herons usually hunt near water, but they also stalk fields and meadows in search of rodents. • Great Blue Herons settle in communal treetop nesting sites called rookeries. Rookeries in Kentucky have contained up to 432 nests and are usually located near the Mississippi or Ohio rivers. Nesting herons are sensitive to human disturbance, so observe this bird's behavior from a distance.

Other ID: blue-gray overall; long, dark legs. *Breeding:* richer colors; plumes streak from crown and throat. *In flight:* black upperwing tips; legs trail behind body; slow, steady wingbeats.
Size: L 4¼–4½ ft; W 6 ft.
Voice: quiet away from the nest; occasional harsh *frahnk frahnk frahnk* during takeoff.
Status: fairly common permanent resident.
Habitat: forages along edges of rivers, lakes and marshes; also fields and wet meadows.

Similar Birds

Little Blue Heron

Sandhill Crane
(p. 56)

Great Egret

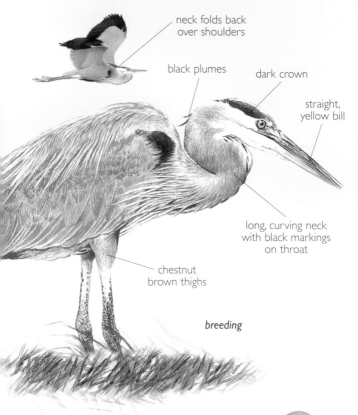

neck folds back over shoulders

black plumes

dark crown

straight, yellow bill

long, curving neck with black markings on throat

chestnut brown thighs

breeding

Nesting: colonial; near water; adds to stick platform nest over years; nest width can reach 4 ft; pale bluish green eggs are 2½ x 1¾ in; pair incubates 4–7 eggs for approximately 28 days.

Did You Know?

The Great Blue Heron is the tallest of all herons and egrets in North America.

Look For

In flight, the Great Blue Heron folds its neck back over its shoulders in an S-shape. Similar-looking cranes stretch their necks out when flying.

Green Heron
Butorides virescens

Sentinel of the marshes, the ever-vigilant Green Heron sits hunched on a shaded branch at the water's edge. This crow-sized heron stalks frogs and small fish lurking in the weedy shallows, then stabs prey with its bill. • Unlike most herons, the Green Heron nests singly rather than communally, though it can sometimes be found in loose colonies. While some of this heron's habitat has been lost to wetland drainage or channelization in the southern states, the building of farm ponds or reservoirs has created habitat in other areas.

Other ID: stocky body; relatively short, yellow-green legs; long bill is dark above and greenish below; short tail. *Breeding male:* bright orange legs.
Size: L 15–22 in; W 26 in.
Voice: generally silent; alarm and flight call are a loud *kowp, kyow* or *skow*; aggression call is a harsh *raah*.
Status: fairly common migrant and summer resident; rare in winter.
Habitat: marshes, lakes and streams with dense shoreline or emergent vegetation.

Similar Birds

Black-crowned
Night-Heron (p. 42)

Least Bittern

American Bittern

dark, iridescent back

dark crown

chestnut face and neck

Nesting: nests singly or in small, loose groups; stick platform in a tree or shrub, usually close to water; blue-green to green eggs are 1½ x 1⅛ in; pair incubates 3–5 eggs for 19–21 days.

Did You Know?

Green Herons sometimes bait fish to the surface by dropping small bits of debris such as twigs, vegetation or feathers.

Look For

The scientific name *virescens* is Latin for "growing or becoming green" and refers to this bird's transition from a streaky brown juvenile to a greenish adult.

Black-crowned Night-Heron

Nycticorax nycticorax

When dusk's long shadows shroud the marshes, the Black-crowned Night-Herons arrive to hunt in the marshy waters. These herons crouch motionless, using their large, light-sensitive eyes to spot prey lurking in the shallows. • Black-crowned Night-Herons are widespread and breed throughout much of the U.S., including a colony on the grounds of the Louisville Zoo. Watch for them in summer between dawn and dusk, as they fly from nesting colonies to feeding areas and back.

Other ID: stocky body; black back; gray neck and wings; dull yellow legs; stout, black bill.
Size: L 23–26 in; W 3½ ft.
Voice: deep, guttural *quark* or *wok,* often heard as the bird takes flight.
Status: uncommon migrant and summer resident in western Kentucky.
Habitat: shallow cattail and bulrush marshes, lakeshores and along slow-flowing rivers.

Similar Birds

Yellow-crowned Night-Heron

Green Heron (p. 40)

American Bittern

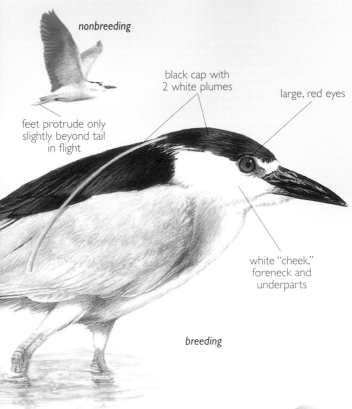

nonbreeding

feet protrude only
slightly beyond tail
in flight

black cap with
2 white plumes

large, red eyes

white "cheek,"
foreneck and
underparts

breeding

Nesting: colonial; in a tree or shrub; male gathers nest material; female builds a loose nest platform of twigs and sticks and lines it with finer materials; pale green eggs are 2¼ x 1 in; pair incubates 3–4 eggs for 21–26 days.

Did You Know?

Nycticorax, meaning "night raven," refers to this bird's distinctive nighttime calls.

Look For

To distinguish Black-crowned Night-Herons in flight, look at their feet, which are shorter than other herons and project only partially beyond the tail.

Turkey Vulture
Cathartes aura

Turkey Vultures are intelligent, playful and social birds. Groups live and sleep together in large trees, or "roosts." Some roost sites are over a century old and have been used by the same family of vultures for several generations. • The genus name *Cathartes* means "cleanser" and refers to this bird's affinity for carrion. A vulture's bill and feet are much less powerful than those of eagles, hawks or falcons, which kill live prey. Its red, featherless head may appear grotesque, but this adaptation allows the bird to stay relatively clean while feeding on messy carcasses.

Other ID: *Immature:* gray head. *In flight:* head appears small; rocks from side to side when soaring.
Size: L 25–31 in; W 5½–6 ft.
Voice: generally silent; occasionally produces a hiss or grunt if threatened.
Status: common summer resident; uncommon winter resident.
Habitat: usually flies over open country, shorelines or roads, rarely over forests.

Similar Birds

Black Vulture

Golden Eagle

Bald Eagle (p. 46)

silver gray flight
feathers

bare, red head

holds wing in
a shallow "V"

brownish black overall

pale,
hooked bill

Nesting: in a cave, crevice, log or among boulders;
uses no nest material; darkly marked, dull white
eggs are 2¾ x 2 in; pair incubates 2 eggs for up
to 41 days.

Did You Know?

A threatened Turkey
Vulture may play dead or
throw up. The odor of its
vomit repulses attackers,
much like the odor of a
skunk's spray.

Look For

No other bird uses updrafts
and thermals in flight as well
as the Turkey Vulture. Pilots
have reported seeing vul-
tures soaring at 20,000 ft.

Bald Eagle

Haliaeetus leucocephalus

This majestic sea eagle hunts mostly fish and is often found near water. While soaring hundreds of feet high in the air, an eagle can spot fish swimming underwater and small rodents scurrying through the grass. Eagles also scavenge carrion and steal food from other birds. • Bald Eagles

immature

do not mature until their fourth or fifth year—only then do they develop the characteristic white head and tail plumage.

Other ID: *1st-year:* dark overall; dark bill; some white in underwings. *2nd-year:* dark "bib"; white in underwings. *3rd-year:* mostly white plumage; yellow at base of bill; yellow eyes. *4th-year:* light head with dark facial streak; variable pale and dark plumage; yellow bill; paler eyes.

Size: *L* 30–43 in; *W* 5½–8 ft.

Voice: thin, weak squeal or gull-like cackle: *kleek-kik-kik-kik* or *kah-kah-kah*.

Status: uncommon migrant and summer resident; increasingly common winter resident; remains on Federally Threatened list.

Habitat: large lakes and rivers.

Similar Birds

Golden Eagle

Osprey

white head
and tail

yellow bill

yellow feet

Nesting: in a tree; usually, but not always, near water; huge stick nest is often reused for many years; white eggs are 2¾ x 2⅛ in; pair incubates 1–3 eggs for 34–36 days.

Did You Know?

The Bald Eagle, a symbol of freedom, longevity and strength, became the emblem of the United States in 1782.

Look For

Bald Eagles mate for life and renew pair bonds by adding sticks to their nests, which can be up to 15 ft in diameter, the largest of any North American bird.

Broad-winged Hawk
Buteo platypterus

The best time to see Broad-winged Hawks in Kentucky is during fall migration, when "kettles" of these buteos follow the Appalachian Mountain range south to wintering grounds in Central and South America. Hundreds or even thousands of these hawks take advantage of warm, thermal air currents to soar, sometimes gliding for hours without flapping. • This shy hawk shuns open fields and forest clearings, preferring dense, often wet forests. In this habitat, its short, broad wings and highly flexible tail help it to maneuver in the heavy growth.

Other ID: broad wings with pointed tips; dark brown upperparts. *Dark morph:* rare; dark brown overall; dark underwing coverts in flight.
Size: *L* 14–19 in; *W* 32–39 in.
Voice: high-pitched, whistled *peeeo-wee-ee*; generally silent during migration.
Status: fairly common migrant and summer resident.
Habitat: *Breeding:* dense mixed and deciduous woodlands. *In migration:* escarpments and shorelines; also riparian and deciduous forests and woodland edges.

Similar Birds

Red-shouldered Hawk

Red-tailed Hawk
(p. 50)

dark "mustache" stripe

pale underwings outlined with dark brown

broad, black and white tail bands

Nesting: usually in a deciduous tree, often near water; bulky stick nest; usually builds a new nest each year; brown-spotted, whitish eggs are 2 x 1½ in; mostly the female incubates 2–4 eggs for 28–31 days; both adults raise the young.

Did You Know?

Of all the raptors, the Broad-winged Hawk is the most likely to be seen clutching a snake.

Look For

Most hunting is done from a high perch with a good view. When flushed, the Broad-winged Hawk will often return to the same perch.

Red-tailed Hawk
Buteo jamaicensis

Take an afternoon drive through the country and look for Red-tailed Hawks soaring above the fields. Red-tails are the most common hawks in Kentucky, especially in winter. • In warm weather, these hawks use thermals and updrafts to soar. The pockets of rising air provide substantial lift, which allows migrating hawks to fly for almost 2 miles without flapping their wings. On cooler days, resident Red-tails perch on exposed tree limbs, fence posts or utility poles to scan for prey.

Other ID: brown eyes; overall color varies geographically. *In flight:* light underwing flight feathers with faint barring; dark leading edge on underside of wings.
Size: *Male: L* 18–23 in; W 4–5 ft. *Female: L* 20–25 in; W 4–5 ft.
Voice: powerful, descending scream: *keeearrrr.*
Status: common permanent resident.
Habitat: open country with some trees; also roadsides or woodlots.

Similar Birds

Broad-winged Hawk
(p. 48)

Red-shouldered Hawk

Rough-legged Hawk

dark "shoulder" patches

dark upperparts with some white highlights

red tail

dark brown band of streaks across belly

Nesting: in woodlands adjacent to open habitat; bulky stick nest is enlarged each year; brown-blotched, whitish eggs are 2⅜ x 1⅞ in; pair incubates 2–4 eggs for 28–35 days.

Did You Know?

The Red-tailed Hawk's piercing call is often paired with the image of an eagle in TV commercials and movies.

Look For

Courting pairs sometimes dive at each other, lock talons and tumble toward the earth. They break away at the last second to avoid crashing into the ground.

American Kestrel
Falco sparverius

The colorful American Kestrel, formerly known as the "Sparrow Hawk," is a common and widespread falcon, not shy of human activity and adaptable to habitat change. This small falcon has benefited from the grassy right-of-ways created by interstate highways, which provide habitat for grasshoppers and other small prey. Watch for this robin-sized bird along rural roadways, perched on poles and telephone wires, or hovering over agricultural fields, foraging for insects and small mammals.

Other ID: lightly spotted underparts. *In flight:* frequently hovers; buoyant, indirect flight style.
Size: L 7½–8 in; W 20–24 in.
Voice: usually silent; loud, often repeated, shrill *killy-killy-killy* when excited; female's voice is lower pitched.
Status: common permanent resident.
Habitat: open fields, riparian wood-lands, woodlots, forest edges, bogs, roadside ditches, grassy highway medians, grasslands and croplands.

Similar Birds

Merlin

Sharp-shinned Hawk

Peregrine Falcon

2 distinctive facial stripes

rusty wings and breast streaking

rusty barring on back

blue-gray crown with rusty cap

♀

♂

blue-gray wings

long, rusty tail

Nesting: in a tree cavity; may use a nest box; white to pale brown, speckled eggs are 1½ x 1⅛ in; mostly the female incubates 4–6 eggs for 29–30 days; both adults raise the young.

Did You Know?

No stranger to captivity, the American Kestrel was the first falcon to reproduce by artificial insemination.

Look For

The American Kestrel repeatedly lifts its tail while perched to scout below for prey.

American Coot
Fulica americana

American Coots resemble ducks but are actually more closely related to rails and gallinules. Coots appear on our lakes, reservoirs and wetlands from September to May. During winter they remain aggressive and territorial, running along the surface of the water and charging intruders. Confrontational coots will stab with their bill while trying to grab the perpetrator with one clawed foot. • With feet that have individually webbed toes, the coot is adapted to diving, but it isn't afraid to snatch a meal from another skilled diver.

Other ID: red eyes; long, yellow-green legs; lobed toes.
Size: *L* 13–16 in; W 24 in.
Voice: calls frequently in summer, day and night: *kuk-kuk-kuk-kuk-kuk;* also croaks and grunts.
Status: common in migration and winter; rare in summer.
Habitat: shallow marshes, ponds and wetlands with open water and emergent vegetation; also sewage lagoons.

Similar Birds

Purple Gallinule

Common Moorhen

Pied-billed Grebe
(p. 36)

reddish spot on white forehead "shield"

white, chickenlike bill with dark ring around tip

white marks on tail

gray-black overall

Nesting: in emergent vegetation; pair builds floating nest of cattails and grass; buffy white, brown-spotted eggs are 2 x 1⅜ in; pair incubates 8–12 eggs for 21–25 days; may raise 2 broods.

Did You Know?

American Coots are the most widespread and abundant rails in North America.

Look For

Though it somewhat resembles a duck, an American Coot bobs its head while swimming or walking and has a narrower bill that extends up the forehead.

Sandhill Crane
Grus canadensis

The Sandhill Crane's deep, rattling call can be heard long before this bird passes overhead. Its coiled trachea alters the pitch of its voice, making it sound louder and carry farther. • At first glance, large, V-shaped flocks of Sandhill Cranes look like flocks of Canada Geese, but the cranes often soar and circle in the air, and they do not honk like geese. • Cranes mate for life and reinforce pair bonds each spring with an elaborate courtship dance. The ritual looks much like human dancing, which may seem a strange comparison until you witness the spectacle firsthand. • Look for these birds in cornfields along river valleys.

Other ID: long, straight bill; dark legs.
Size: *L* 3¼–4¼ ft; *W* 6–7 ft.
Voice: loud, resonant, rattling: *gu-rrroo gu-rrroo gurrroo*.
Status: uncommon migrant.
Habitat: *Breeding:* isolated, open marshes, fens and bogs lined with trees or shrubs. *In migration:* agricultural fields, sandbars and shorelines.

Similar Birds

Great Blue Heron
(p. 38)

Whooping Crane

naked, red crown

long neck is held straight in flight

white "cheek" and "chin"

gray plumage is often stained rusty red from iron oxides in the water

Nesting: does not nest in Kentucky; nests in the Arctic; in the water or along a shoreline; on a large mound of aquatic vegetation; brown-blotched, buff eggs are 3¾ x 2⅜ in; pair incubates 2 eggs for 29–32 days.

Did You Know?

Flocks of migrating Sandhill Cranes are usually made up of close family members.

Look For

Especially in fall, Sandhills migrate over central Kentucky, south and west of Louisville. Whooping Cranes are increasingly seen with the Sandhills during migration.

Killdeer
Charadrius vociferus

The Killdeer is a gifted actor, well known for its "broken wing" distraction display. When an intruder wanders too close to its nest, the Killdeer greets the interloper with piteous cries while dragging a wing and stumbling about as if injured. Most predators take the bait and follow, and once the Killdeer has lured the predator far away from its nest, it miraculously recovers from the injury and flies off with a loud call.

Other ID: brown head; white neck band; brown back and upperwings; white underparts; rufous rump. *Immature:* downy; only 1 breast band.
Size: L 9–11 in; W 24 in.
Voice: loud, distinctive *kill-dee kill-dee kill-deer;* variations include *deer-deer*.
Status: common permanent resident.
Habitat: open areas, such as fields, lakeshores, sandy beaches, mudflats, gravel streambeds, wet meadows and grasslands.

Similar Birds

Semipalmated Plover

Look For

The Killdeer has adapted well to urbanization, and it finds golf courses, farms, fields and abandoned industrial areas as much to its liking as shorelines.

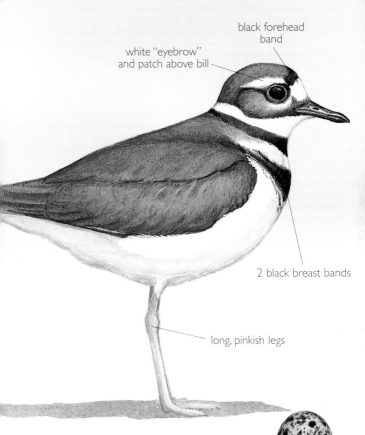

white "eyebrow" and patch above bill

black forehead band

2 black breast bands

long, pinkish legs

Nesting: on open ground; in a shallow, usually unlined depression; heavily marked, creamy buff eggs are 1⅜ x 1⅛ in; pair incubates 4 eggs for 24–28 days; may raise 2 broods.

Did You Know?

The scientific name *vociferus* aptly describes this vocal bird. In spring, you might hear a European Starling imitate the Killdeer's call.

Lesser Yellowlegs
Tringa flavipes

The "tattletale" Lesser Yellowlegs is the self-appointed sentinel in a mixed flock of shorebirds, raising the alarm at the first sign of a threat. • It is challenging to discern Lesser Yellowlegs and Greater Yellowlegs (*T. melanoleuca*) in the field, but with practice, you will notice that the Lesser's bill is finer, straighter and shorter, about as long as its head is wide. With its long legs and wings, the Lesser appears slimmer and taller than the Greater, and it is more commonly seen in flocks. Finally, the Lesser Yellowlegs emits a pair of peeps, while the Greater Yellowlegs peeps three times.

Other ID: subtle, dark eye line; pale lores; brown-black mottling on upperparts. *Nonbreeding:* grayer overall.
Size: *L* 10–11 in; W 24 in.
Voice: typically a high-pitched pair of *tew* notes; noisiest on breeding grounds.
Status: common migrant.
Habitat: shorelines of lakes, rivers, marshes and ponds.

Similar Birds

| Willet | Greater Yellowlegs | Solitary Sandpiper |

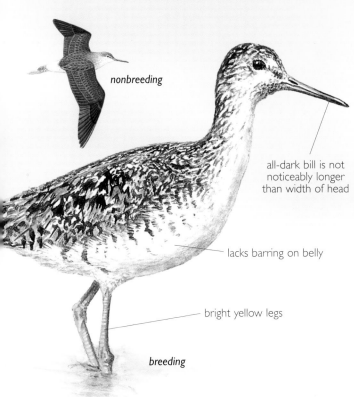

nonbreeding

all-dark bill is not noticeably longer than width of head

lacks barring on belly

bright yellow legs

breeding

Nesting: does not nest in Kentucky; nests in the Arctic; in a natural forest opening; in a depression on a dry mound lined with leaves and grass; darkly blotched, buff to olive eggs are 1⅝ x 1⅛ in; pair incubates 4 eggs for 22–23 days.

Did You Know?

Yellowlegs were popular game birds in the 1800s because they were plentiful and easy to shoot.

Look For

When feeding, the Lesser Yellowlegs wades into water almost to its belly, sweeping its bill back and forth just below the water's surface.

Spotted Sandpiper

Actitis macularius

The female Spotted Sandpiper, unlike most other female birds, lays her eggs and leaves the male to tend the clutch. She diligently defends her territory and may mate with several different males. Only about one percent of birds display this unusual breeding strategy known as "polyandry." Each summer, the female can lay up to four clutches and is capable of producing 20 eggs. As the season progresses, however, available males become harder to find. Come August, there may be seven females for every available male.

Other ID: *Nonbreeding* and *immature:* pure white breast, foreneck and throat; brown bill; dull yellow legs. *In flight:* flies close to the water's surface with very rapid, shallow, stiff-winged strokes.
Size: *L* 7–8 in; *W* 15 in.
Voice: sharp, crisp *eat-wheat, eat-wheat, wheat-wheat-wheat-wheat.*
Status: common migrant.
Habitat: shorelines, gravel beaches, drainage ditches, swamps and sewage lagoons; occasionally seen in cultivated fields.

Similar Birds

Solitary Sandpiper

Dunlin

long tail

breeding

short, white
upperwing stripe

dark eye line

white "eyebrow"

black-tipped,
yellow-orange bill

white underparts heavily
spotted with black

yellow-orange legs

breeding

Nesting: rarely nests in Kentucky; usually near water; shallow scrape is lined with grass and sheltered by vegetation; darkly blotched, creamy buff eggs are 1¼ x 1 in; male incubates 4 eggs for 20–24 days.

Did You Know?

Sandpipers have four toes: three pointing forward and one pointing backward. Plovers such as the Killdeer have only three toes.

Look For

Spotted Sandpipers bob their tails constantly on shore, and teeter almost continuously.

Ring-billed Gull

Larus delawarensis

Few people can claim that they have never seen this common and widespread gull. Highly tolerant of humans, Ring-billed Gulls are part of our everyday lives, scavenging our litter and fouling our parks. These omnivorous gulls will eat almost anything and will swarm parks, beaches, golf courses and fast-food parking lots looking for food handouts, making pests of themselves. However, few species have adjusted to human development as well as the Ring-billed Gull, which is something to appreciate.

Other ID: *Breeding:* white head and upperparts. *In flight:* pale gray mantle.
Size: L 18–20 in; W 4 ft.
Voice: high-pitched *kakakaka-akakaka;* also a low, laughlike *yook-yook-yook.*
Status: common migrant and winter resident.
Habitat: *Breeding:* bare, rocky and shrubby islands and sewage ponds. *In migration* and *winter:* lakes, rivers, landfills, golf courses, large parking lots, fields and parks.

Similar Birds

Herring Gull

California Gull

black wing tips with
a few white spots

nonbreeding

yellow eyes

black ring around
bill tip

yellow bill

yellow legs

nonbreeding

Nesting: does not nest in Kentucky; nests in northern U.S. and Canada; colonial; in a shallow scrape on the ground, lined with grass, debris and small sticks; brown-blotched, gray to olive eggs are 2⅜ x 1⅝ in; pair incubates 2–4 eggs for 23–28 days.

Did You Know?

In chaotic nesting colonies, adult Ring-billed Gulls will call out for their young and can recognize the response of their chicks.

Look For

To differentiate between gulls, pay attention to the markings on their bills and the color of their legs and eyes.

Rock Pigeon
Columba livia

Rock Pigeons are familiar to most anyone who has lived in the city. These colorful, acrobatic, seed-eating birds frequent parks, town squares, railroad yards and factory sites. Their tolerance of humans has made them a source of entertainment, as well as a pest. • This pigeon is likely a descendant of a Eurasian bird that was first domesticated about 4500 BC. The Rock Pigeon was introduced to North America in the 17th century by settlers.

Other ID: *In flight:* holds wings in a deep "V" while gliding.
Size: *L* 12–13 in; *W* 28 in (male is usually larger).
Voice: soft, cooing *coorrr-coorrr-coorrr.*
Status: common permanent resident.
Habitat: urban areas, railroad yards and agricultural areas; high cliffs often provide a more natural habitat for some.

Similar Birds

Mourning Dove
(p. 68)

Eurasian
Collared-Dove

color is highly variable
(iridescent, blue-gray,
red, white or tan)

white
cere

usually has
white rump

feet usually
orangy red

dark-tipped tail

Nesting: in a barn or on a cliff, bridge or tower; in a flimsy nest of sticks, grass and other vegetation; glossy white eggs are 1½ x 1⅛ in; pair incubates 2 eggs for 16–19 days; may raise broods year-round.

Did You Know?

Much of our understanding of bird migration, endocrinology and color genetics comes from experiments involving Rock Pigeons.

Look For

No other "wild" bird varies as much in coloration, a result of semidomestication and extensive inbreeding over time.

Mourning Dove
Zenaida macroura

The Mourning Dove's soft cooing, which filters through broken woodlands and suburban parks, is often confused with the sound of a hooting owl. Beginning birders who track down the source of the calls are often surprised to find the streamlined silhouette of a perched dove. • This popular game animal is common throughout Kentucky and is one of the most abundant native birds in North America. Its numbers and range have increased since human development created more open habitats and food sources, such as waste grain and bird feeders.

Other ID: buffy, gray-brown plumage; small head; dark bill; sleek body; dull red legs.
Size: *L* 11–13 in; *W* 18 in.
Voice: mournful, soft, slow *oh-woe-woe-woe*.
Status: common permanent resident.
Habitat: open and riparian woodlands, forest edges, agricultural and suburban areas, open parks.

Similar Birds

Rock Pigeon
(p. 66)

Eurasian
Collared-Dove

pale blue eye ring

dark, shiny patch below ear

long, white-trimmed, tapering tail

pale rosy underparts

black spots on upperwings

Nesting: in a shrub or tree; occasionally on the ground; nest is a fragile, shallow platform of twigs; white eggs are $1\frac{1}{8}$ x $\frac{7}{8}$ in; pair incubates 2 eggs for 14 days.

Did You Know?

Mourning Doves raise up to six broods each year—more than any other native bird.

Look For

When the Mourning Dove bursts into flight, its wings clap above and below its body. It also often creates a whistling sound as it flies at high speed.

Yellow-billed Cuckoo
Coccyzus americanus

Large tracts of hardwood forest with plenty of clearings, such as Land Between the Lakes, provide valuable habitat for the Yellow-billed Cuckoo, a bird that is declining over much of its range and has already disappeared in some states. The cuckoo's habitat has also steadily disappearing as waterways are altered or dammed. • The cuckoo skillfully negotiates its tangled home within impenetrable, deciduous undergrowth in silence, relying on obscurity for survival. Then, for a short period during nesting, the male cuckoo tempts fate by issuing a barrage of loud, rhythmic courtship calls.

Other ID: olive brown upperparts; white underparts.
Size: L 11–13 in; W 18 in.
Voice: long series of deep, hollow *kuks*, slowing near the end: *kuk-kuk-kuk-kuk kuk kop kow kowlp kowlp*.
Status: fairly common migrant and summer resident.
Habitat: semi-open deciduous habitats; dense tangles and thickets at the edges of orchards, urban parks, agricultural fields and roadways; sometimes woodlots.

Similar Birds

Black-billed Cuckoo

Mourning Dove
(p. 68)

yellow eye ring

rufous tinge
on primaries

mainly yellow,
downcurved bill with
black upper ridge

long tail with large
white spots on
underside

Nesting: on a low horizontal branch in a deciduous shrub or small tree, flimsy platform nest of twigs is lined with grass; pale bluish green eggs are 1¼ x ⅞ in; pair incubates 3–4 eggs for 9–11 days.

Did You Know?

Yellow-billed Cuckoos lay larger clutches when cyclical outbreaks of cicadas or tent caterpillars provide an abundant food supply.

Look For

The Yellow-billed Cuckoo, or "Rain Crow," has a propensity for calling on dark, cloudy days and a reputation for predicting rainstorms.

Eastern Screech-Owl
Megascops asio

red morph

The diminutive Eastern Screech-Owl is a year-round resident of low-elevation, deciduous woodlands, but its presence is rarely detected—most screech-owls sleep away the daylight hours. • The noise of a mobbing horde of chickadees or a squawking gang of Blue Jays can alert you to an owl's presence during the day. Smaller birds that mob a screech-owl often do so after losing a family member during the night. • Unique among Kentucky owls, Eastern Screech-Owls show both red and gray color morphs. In Kentucky, the gray morph is more common. Very rarely, an intermediate brown morph occurs.

Other ID: reddish or grayish overall; yellow eyes.
Size: L 8–9 in; W 20–22 in.
Voice: horselike "whinny" that rises and falls.
Status: fairly common permanent resident.
Habitat: mature deciduous forests, open deciduous and riparian woodlands, orchards and shade trees with natural cavities.

Similar Birds

Northern Saw-whet
Owl

Long-eared Owl

short "ear" tufts

pale
grayish
bill

dark breast
streaking

gray morph

Nesting: in a natural cavity or artificial nest box; no lining is added; white eggs are 1½ x 1⅜ in; female incubates 4–5 eggs for about 26 days; male brings food to the female during incubation.

Did You Know?

Screech-owls have a varied diet that includes small animals, earthworms, insects and sometimes even fish.

Look For

Eastern Screech-Owls respond readily to whistled imitations of their calls, and sometimes several owls will appear to investigate the fraudulent perpetrator.

Great Horned Owl
Bubo virginianus

This highly adaptable and superbly camouflaged hunter has sharp hearing and powerful vision that allow it to hunt at night as well as by day. It will swoop down from a perch onto almost any small creature that moves. • An owl has specially designed feathers on its wings to reduce noise. The leading edge of the flight feathers is fringed rather than smooth, which interrupts airflow over the wing and allows the owl to fly noiselessly. • Great Horned Owls begin their courtship as early as January, and by February and March the females are already incubating their eggs.

Other ID: overall plumage varies from light gray to dark brown; heavily mottled, gray, brown and black upperparts; yellow eyes; white "chin."
Size: *L* 18–25 in; *W* 3–5 ft.
Voice: breeding call is 4–6 deep hoots: *hoo-hoo-hoooo hoo-hoo* or *Who's awake? Me too;* female gives higher-pitched hoots.
Status: fairly common permanent resident.
Habitat: fragmented forests, fields, riparian woodlands, suburban parks and wooded edges of clearings.

Similar Birds

Barred Owl

Short-eared Owl

Long-eared Owl

tall, widely spaced
"ear" tufts form a
triangle with beak

rusty orange facial
disc is outlined in
black

fine, horizontal
barring on breast

Nesting: in another bird's abandoned stick nest
or in a tree cavity; adds little or no nest material;
dull whitish eggs are 2¼ x 1⅞ in; mostly the
female incubates 2–3 eggs for 28–35 days.

Did You Know?

The Great Horned Owl
has a poor sense of smell,
which might explain why
it is the only consistent
predator of skunks.

Look For

Owls regurgitate pellets that
contain the indigestible parts
of their prey. You can find
these pellets, which are generally clean and dry, under
frequently used perches.

Common Nighthawk
Chordeiles minor

The Common Nighthawk makes an unforgettable booming sound as it flies high overhead. In an energetic courting display, the male dives, then swerves skyward, making a hollow *vroom* sound with its wings. • Like other members of the nightjar family, the Common Nighthawk has adapted to catch insects in midair: its large, gaping mouth is surrounded by feather shafts that funnel insects into its bill. A nighthawk can eat over 2600 insects in one day, including mosquitoes, blackflies and flying ants. • Look for nighthawks foraging for insects at nighttime baseball games.

Other ID: *In flight:* shallowly forked, barred tail; erratic flight.
Size: L 8–10 in; W 23–26 in.
Voice: frequently repeated, nasal *peent peent*.
Status: fairly common summer resident.
Habitat: *Breeding:* forest openings, bogs, rocky outcroppings and gravel rooftops. *In migration:* often near water; any area with large numbers of flying insects.

Similar Birds

Chuck-will's-widow

Whip-poor-will
(p. 78)

bold, white "wrist" patches on long, painted wings

very small bill

cryptic, mottled plumage

♂

barred underparts

white throat (buff on female)

Nesting: on bare ground; no nest is built; heavily marked, creamy white to buff eggs are 1⅛ x ⅞ in; female incubates 2 eggs for about 19 days; both adults feed the young.

Did You Know?

It was once believed that members of the nightjar, or "goatsucker," family could suck milk from the udders of goats, causing the goats to go blind!

Look For

With their short legs and tiny feet, nighthawks sit lengthwise on tree branches and blend in perfectly with the bark. This bird is called the "Bullbat" by some.

Whip-poor-will
Caprimulgus vociferus

These magical, elusive birds blend seamlessly into lichen-covered bark or the forest floor. On spring evenings, their airy, soothing *whip-poor-will* calls float through the open woodlands, signaling to prospective mates. • Ground-nesting Whip-poor-wills time their egg-laying to the lunar cycle so that hatchlings can be fed more efficiently during the light of the full moon. For the first 20 days after hatching, until the young are able to fly, the parents feed them regurgitated insects.

Other ID: mottled, brown gray overall with black flecking; large eyes; dark throat; relatively long, rounded tail. *Red morph:* mottled, rufous overall; pale gray markings on wings.
Size: *L* 9–10 in; *W* 16–20 in.
Voice: whistled *whip-poor-will*, with emphasis on *will*.
Status: fairly common summer resident.
Habitat: open deciduous and pine woodlands; often along forest edges.

Similar Birds

Chuck-will's-widow

Common Nighthawk
(p. 76)

rounded wings

white outer
tail feathers
(buff on female)

dark stripe runs down
center of crown

dark throat

white "necklace"
(buff on female)

Nesting: on the ground in leaf or pine needle litter; no nest is built; whitish eggs with brown blotches are 1¼ x ⅞ in; female incubates 2 eggs for 19–20 days; both adults raise the young.

Did You Know?

Within days of hatching, young Whip-poor-wills can scurry away from their nest in search of protective cover if disturbed.

Look For

Cryptic plumage, sleepy daytime habits and secretive nesting behavior mean a hopeful observer must literally stumble upon a Whip-poor-will to see one.

Chimney Swift
Chaetura pelagica

Chimney Swifts are the "frequent fliers" of the bird world—they feed, drink, bathe, collect nest material and even mate while they fly! They spend much of their time catching insects in the skies above Kentucky's treetops. During night migrations, swifts sleep as they fly, relying on changing wind conditions to steer them. • Chimney Swifts have small, weak legs and cannot take flight again if they land on the ground. For this reason, swifts usually cling to vertical surfaces with their strong claws.

Other ID: brown overall; slim body. *In flight:* rapid wing-beats; boomerang-shaped profile; erratic flight pattern.
Size: L 5–5½ in; W 12–13 in.
Voice: call is a rapid *chitter-chitter-chitter,* given in flight; also gives a rapid series of staccato *chip* notes.
Status: common migrant and summer resident.
Habitat: forages above cities and towns; roosts and nests in chimneys; may nest in tree cavities in more remote areas.

Similar Birds

Northern Rough-winged Swallow (p. 116)

Bank Swallow

Cliff Swallow

long, thin, pointed, crescent-shaped wings

squared tail

Nesting: often colonial; half-saucer nest of short twigs is attached to a vertical wall using saliva; white eggs are ¾ x ½ in; pair incubates 4–5 eggs for 19–21 days.

Did You Know?

Migrating Chimney Swifts may fly as high as 10,000 feet—above this altitude aircraft are required to carry oxygen.

Look For

In early evenings during migration, Chimney Swifts are often seen in large numbers swirling above large, old chimneys before they enter to roost for the night.

Ruby-throated Hummingbird

Archilochus colubris

Ruby-throated Hummingbirds feed on sweet, energy-rich flower nectar and pollinate flowers in the process. You can attract hummingbirds to your backyard with a red nectar feeder filled with a sugarwater solution (red food coloring is both unnecessary and harmful to the birds) or with native nectar-producing flowers such as honeysuckle or bee balm. • Each year, Ruby-throated Hummingbirds migrate across the Gulf of Mexico—a nonstop, 500-mile journey. Weighing about as much as a nickel, a hummingbird can briefly reach speeds of up to 60 miles per hour.

Other ID: thin, needlelike bill; pale underparts.
Size: *L* 3½–4 in; *W* 4–4½ in.
Voice: a loud *chick* and other high squeaks; soft buzzing of the wings while in flight.
Status: common summer resident.
Habitat: open, mixed woodlands, wetlands, orchards, tree-lined meadows, flower gardens and backyards with trees and feeders.

Similar Birds

Rufous Hummingbird

Black-chinned Hummingbird

iridescent, green back

fine, dark streaking on white throat

black "chin" and ruby red throat

dark tail

Nesting: on a horizontal tree limb; tiny, deep cup nest of plant down and fibers is held together with spider silk; lichens and leaves are pasted on the exterior walls; white eggs are ½ x ⅜ in; female incubates 2 eggs for 13–16 days.

Did You Know?

In straight-ahead flight, hummingbirds beat their wings up to 80 times per second, and their hearts can beat up to 1200 times per minute!

Look For

A hummingbird with a greenish back and white throat is most likely female. Nonbreeding males have dark brown to black throats.

Belted Kingfisher
Ceryle alcyon

Perched on a bare branch over a productive pool, the Belted Kingfisher utters a scratchy, rattling call. Then, with little regard for its scruffy hairdo, the "king of the fishers" plunges headfirst into the water, snatching a fish or a frog. Back on land, the kingfisher flips its prey into the air and swallows it headfirst. Similar to owls, kingfishers regurgitate the indigestible portion of their food as pellets, which can be found beneath favorite perches.
• Nestlings have closed eyes and are featherless for the first week, but after five days they are able to swallow small fish whole.

Other ID: bluish upperparts; small, white patch near eye; straight bill; short legs; white underwings.
Size: L 11–14 in; W 20–21 in.
Voice: fast, repetitive, cackling rattle, like a teacup shaking on a saucer.
Status: fairly common permanent resident.
Habitat: rivers, large streams, lakes, marshes and beaver ponds, especially near exposed soil banks, gravel pits or bluffs.

Similar Birds

Blue Jay (p. 110)

Look For

The Belted Kingfisher often flies very close to the water, so close, in fact, that its wing tips may skim the surface.

shaggy crest

white "collar"

♀

rust-colored "belt"
on female may be
incomplete

♂

blue-gray
breast band

Nesting: in a cavity at the end of an earth burrow; glossy white eggs are 1⅜ x 1 in; pair incubates
6–7 eggs for 22–24 days.

Did You Know?

Kingfisher pairs nest on sandy banks near water and use
their sturdy bills and claws to dig burrows that may meas-
ure up to 6 ft long.

Red-headed Woodpecker
Melanerpes erythrocephalus

This bird of the East lives mostly in open deciduous woodlands, urban parks and oak savannahs. Red-heads were once common throughout their range, but their numbers have declined dramatically over the past century. Since the introduction of the European Starling, Red-headed Woodpeckers have been largely outcompeted for nesting cavities.
• These birds are frequent traffic fatalities, often struck by vehicles when they dart from their perches and over roadways to catch flying insects.

Other ID: black tail; white underparts. *Juvenile:* brown head, back, wings and tail; slight brown streaking on white underparts.
Size: *L* 9–9½ in; *W* 17 in.
Voice: loud series of *kweer* or *kwrring* notes; occasionally a chattering *kerr-r-ruck;* also drums softly in short bursts.
Status: fairly common permanent resident.
Habitat: open deciduous woodlands (especially oak woodlands), urban parks, river edges and roadsides with groves of scattered trees.

Similar Birds

Red-bellied Woodpecker (p. 88)

Pileated Woodpecker (p. 94)

bright red head

black back and wings

all-white rump and innerwing patches

juvenile

large, white wing patches

Nesting: male excavates a nest cavity in a dead tree or limb; white eggs are 1 x ¾ in; pair incubates 4–5 eggs for 12–13 days; both adults feed the young.

Did You Know?

The Red-headed Woodpecker is one of only four woodpecker species that caches food.

Look For

The forested bottomlands, swamps and semi-open habitats of western Kentucky are favorite haunts of the charismatic Red-headed Woodpecker.

Red-bellied Woodpecker
Melanerpes carolinus

The familiar Red-bellied Woodpecker is no stranger to suburban backyards and will sometimes nest in birdhouses. This widespread bird is found year-round in woodlands throughout the eastern states, but numbers fluctuate depending on habitat availability and weather conditions. • Unlike most woodpeckers, Red-bellies consume large amounts of plant material, seldom excavating wood for insects. • When occupying an area together with Red-headed Woodpeckers, Red-bellies will nest in the trunk, below the foliage, and the Red-heads will nest in dead branches among the foliage.

Other ID: reddish tinge on belly. *Juvenile:* dark gray crown; streaked breast.
Size: *L* 9–10½ in; *W* 16 in.
Voice: call is a soft, rolling *churr;* drums in second-long bursts.
Status: common permanent resident.
Habitat: mature deciduous woodlands; occasionally in wooded residential areas.

Similar Birds

Northern Flicker
(p. 92)

Red-headed
Woodpecker (p. 86)

Yellow-bellied
Sapsucker

red nape extends
to forehead

black and white
barring on back

♂

red nape

♀

white patches
on rump

Nesting: in a cavity excavated by mainly by the male; nest in woodlands or residential areas; white eggs are 1 x ¾ in; pair incubates 4–5 eggs for 12–14 days.

Did You Know?

Studies of banded Red-bellied Woodpeckers have shown that these birds have a lifespan in the wild of more than 20 years.

Look For

The Red-bellied Woodpecker's namesake, its red belly, is only a small reddish area that is difficult to see in the field.

Downy Woodpecker
Picoides pubescens

A bird feeder well stocked with peanut butter and black-oil sunflower seeds may attract a pair of Downy Woodpeckers to your backyard. These approachable little birds are more tolerant of human activity than most other species, and they visit feeders more often than the larger, more aggressive Hairy Woodpeckers *(P. villosus).* • Like other woodpeckers, the Downy has evolved special features to help cushion the shock of repeated hammering, including a strong bill and neck muscles, a flexible, reinforced skull and a brain that is tightly packed in its protective cranium.

Other ID: black eye line and crown; white belly. *Male:* small, red patch on back of head. *Female:* no red patch.
Size: *L* 6–7 in; *W* 12 in.
Voice: long, unbroken trill; calls are a sharp *pik* or *ki-ki-ki* or whiny *queek queek.*
Status: common permanent resident.
Habitat: any wooded environment, especially deciduous and mixed forests and areas with tall, deciduous shrubs.

Similar Birds

Hairy Woodpecker

Look For

The Downy Woodpecker uses its small bill to probe tiny crevices for invertebrates and wood-boring grubs.

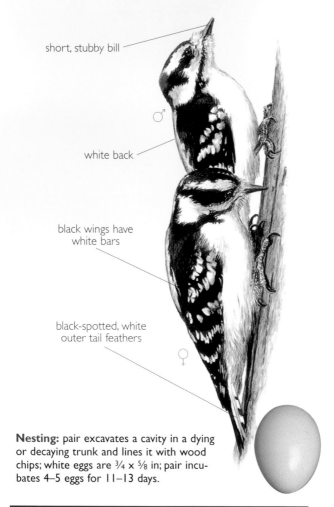

short, stubby bill

♂

white back

black wings have
white bars

black-spotted, white
outer tail feathers

♀

Nesting: pair excavates a cavity in a dying
or decaying trunk and lines it with wood
chips; white eggs are ¾ x ⅝ in; pair incubates 4–5 eggs for 11–13 days.

Did You Know?

Woodpeckers have feathered nostrils, which filter out the
sawdust produced by hammering. When they excavate,
woodpeckers close their eyes just before the bill makes
contact with the tree.

Northern Flicker
Colaptes auratus

Instead of boring holes in trees, the Northern Flicker scours the ground in search of invertebrates, particularly ants. With robinlike hops, it investigates anthills, grassy meadows and forest clearings. • Flickers often bathe in dusty depressions. The dust particles absorb oils and bacteria that can harm the birds' feathers. To clean themselves even more thoroughly, flickers squash ants and preen themselves with the remains. Ants contain formic acid, which kills small parasites on the birds' skin and feathers.

Other ID: long bill; brownish to buff face; gray crown; white rump. *Male:* black "mustache" stripe. *Female:* no "mustache."
Size: L 12–13 in; W 20 in.
Voice: loud, rapid, laughlike *kick-kick-kick-kick-kick-kick; woika-woika-woika* issued during courtship.
Status: common permanent resident; less common in winter.
Habitat: *Breeding:* open woodlands and forest edges, fields, meadows, beaver ponds and other wetlands. *In migration* and *winter:* urban gardens.

Similar Birds

Red-bellied
Woodpecker (p. 88)

Yellow-bellied
Sapsucker

black barring on brown back and wings

red nape crescent

black-spotted, buff to whitish underparts

black "bib"

yellow underwings and undertail

"Yellow-shafted Flicker"

Nesting: pair excavates a cavity in a dying or decaying trunk and lines it with wood chips; may also use a nest box; white eggs are 1⅛ x ⅞ in; pair incubates 5–8 eggs for 11–16 days.

Did You Know?

The very long tongue of a woodpecker wraps around twin structures in the skull and is stored like a measuring tape in its case.

Look For

Northern Flickers prefer to forage at anthills and may visit their favorite colonies regularly, hammering and probing into the ground to unearth adults and larvae.

Pileated Woodpecker
Dryocopus pileatus

The Pileated Woodpecker, with its flaming red crest, chisel-like bill and commanding size, requires 100 acres of mature forest as a home territory. In Kentucky, the patchwork of woodlots and small towns limits the availability of continuous habitat, requiring this woodpecker to show itself more.
• A pair of woodpeckers will spend up to six weeks excavating a large nest cavity in a dead or decaying tree. Wood Ducks, kestrels, owls and even flying squirrels frequently nest in abandoned Pileated Woodpecker cavities.

Other ID: predominantly black; yellow eyes; white "chin." *Male:* red "mustache." *Female:* no red "mustache"; gray-brown forehead.
Size: L 16–17 in; W 28–29 in.
Voice: loud, fast, rolling *woika-woika-woika-woika;* long series of *kuk* notes; loud, resonant drumming.
Status: fairly common permanent resident.
Habitat: extensive tracts of mature forest; also riparian woodlands or woodlots in suburban and agricultural areas.

Similar Birds

Red-headed
Woodpecker (p. 86)

Look For

Foraging Pileated Woodpeckers leave large, rectangular cavities up to 12 inches long at the base of trees.

flaming red crest
extends to bill
on male

♂

stout, dark bill

♀

white stripe
from bill to
shoulder

white wing
linings

Nesting: pair excavates a cavity in a dying or
decaying trunk and lines it with wood chips;
white eggs are 1¼ x 1 in; pair incubates 4 eggs
for 15–18 days.

Did You Know?

The shape of a woodpecker's bill depends on the hardness
of the wood that a species excavates and how hard the
bird hammers. A woodpecker's bill becomes shorter as
the bird ages, so juvenile birds have slightly longer bills
than adults.

Eastern Wood-Pewee
Contopus virens

The Eastern Wood-Pewee is a common and widespread woodland flycatcher that breeds in every county in Kentucky. The male is readily detected by his plaintive, whistled *pee-ah-wee pee-oh* song, which is repeated all day long throughout summer. Some of the keenest suitors will even sing their charms late into the evening. • Many insects have evolved defense mechanisms to avert potential predators such as the Eastern Wood-Pewee and its flycatching relatives. Some flying insects are camouflaged, while others are distasteful or poisonous and flaunt their foul nature with vivid colors.

Other ID: slender body; olive gray to olive brown upperparts; whitish throat; gray breast and sides.
Size: *L* 6–6½ in; *W* 10 in.
Voice: *Male:* song is a clear, slow, plaintive *pee-ah-wee*, with the 2nd note lower, followed by a down-slurred *pee-oh*, with or without intermittent pauses; also a *chip* call.
Status: abundant summer resident.
Habitat: open mixed and deciduous woodlands with a sparse understory, especially openings and edges; rarely in open coniferous woodlands.

Similar Birds

Olive-sided Flycatcher

Eastern Phoebe
(p. 98)

Eastern Kingbird
(p. 102)

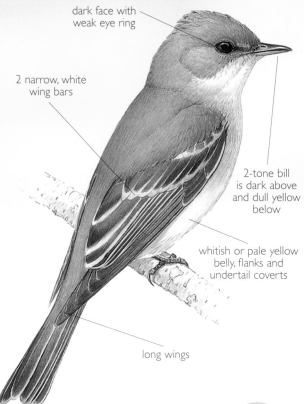

dark face with weak eye ring

2 narrow, white wing bars

2-tone bill is dark above and dull yellow below

whitish or pale yellow belly, flanks and undertail coverts

long wings

Nesting: on a horizontal, deciduous branch, well away from the trunk; open cup nest of plants and lichen is bound with spider silk; whitish, darkly blotched eggs are $^{11}/_{16}$ x $^{9}/_{16}$ in; female incubates 3 eggs for 12–13 days.

Did You Know?

Sometimes you can hear the snap of a wood-pewee's bill closing around an insect.

Look For

The Eastern Wood-Pewee loops out from an exposed perch to snatch flying insects in midair, a technique often referred to as "flycatching" or "hawking."

Acadian Flycatcher
Empidonax virescens

The Acadian Flycatcher's quick, forceful *peet-sa* song is one of its key features, but learning to identify this bird is only half the fun. Its speedy, aerial courtship chases and the male's hovering flight displays are sights to behold—that is if you can survive the swarming hordes of bloodsucking mosquitoes deep within the swampy woodlands where this flycatcher is primarily found. • Maple and beech trees provide preferred nest sites for the Acadian Flycatcher. The nest is built on a horizontal branch up to 20 feet above the ground and can be quite conspicuous because loose material often dangles from the nest.

Other ID: large bill has dark upper mandible and pinkish yellow lower mandible; faint olive yellow breast; yellow belly and undertail coverts.
Size: *L* 5½–6 in; *W* 9 in.
Voice: song is a forceful *peet-sa;* call is a softer *peet;* may issue a loud, flickerlike *ti-ti-ti-ti-ti* during the breeding season.
Status: common summer resident.
Habitat: fairly mature deciduous woodlands, riparian woodlands and wooded swamps.

Similar Birds

Alder Flycatcher

Willow Flycatcher

Least Flycatcher

Yellow-bellied Flycatcher

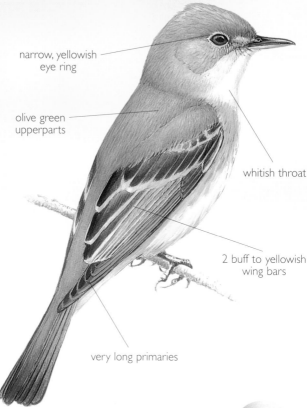

narrow, yellowish eye ring

olive green upperparts

whitish throat

2 buff to yellowish wing bars

very long primaries

Nesting: low in a deciduous tree; female builds a loose cup nest from vegetation held together with spider silk; lightly spotted, creamy white eggs are $^{11}/_{16}$ x $^{9}/_{16}$ in; female incubates 3 eggs for 13–15 days.

Did You Know?

Flycatchers are members of the family Tyrannidae, or "Tyrant Flycatchers," so named because of their feisty, aggressive behavior.

Look For

A standing dead tree or "planted" tree limb in your backyard may attract fly-catchers that are looking for a hunting perch.

Eastern Phoebe
Sayornis phoebe

Whether you are poking around a barnyard, a campground picnic shelter or your backyard shed, there is a very good chance you will stumble upon an Eastern Phoebe family and their marvelous mud nest. The Eastern Phoebe's nest building and territorial defense is normally well underway by the time most other songbirds arrive in Kentucky in mid-May. Once limited to nesting on natural cliffs and fallen riparian trees, this adaptive flycatcher has found success nesting is culverts and under bridges and eaves, especially when water is near.

Other ID: gray brown upperparts; belly may be washed with yellow in fall; no eye ring; weak wing bars; dark legs.
Size: *L* 6½–7 in; *W* 10½ in.
Voice: *Male:* song is a hearty, snappy *fee-bee*, delivered frequently; call is a sharp *chip*.
Status: common summer resident.
Habitat: open deciduous woodlands, forest edges and clearings; usually near water.

Similar Birds

Eastern Wood-Pewee
(p. 96)

Olive-sided Flycatcher

Eastern Kingbird
(p. 104)

dark head and bill

gray wash on breast and sides

white underparts

breeding

frequently pumps its tail

Nesting: under the ledge of a building, picnic shelter, bridge or in a culvert, cliff or well; cup-shaped mud nest is lined with soft material; unmarked, white eggs are ¾ x ⁹⁄₁₆ in; female incubates 4–5 eggs for about 16 days.

Did You Know?

Eastern Phoebes sometimes reuse their nest sites for many years. A female that saves energy by reusing her nest is often able to lay more eggs.

Look For

Some other birds pump their tails while perched, but few species can match the zest and frequency of the Eastern Phoebe's tail pumping.

Great Crested Flycatcher

Myiarchus crinitus

Loud, raucous calls give away the presence of the brightly colored Great Crested Flycatcher. This large flycatcher often inhabits forest edges and nests in woodlands throughout Kentucky. Unlike other eastern flycatchers, the Great Crested prefers to nest in a tree cavity or abandoned woodpecker hole, or sometimes uses a nest box intended for a bluebird. Once in a while, the Great Crested Flycatcher will decorate the nest entrance with a shed snakeskin or substitute translucent plastic wrap. The purpose of this practice is not fully understood, though it might make any would-be predators think twice.

Other ID: dark olive brown upperparts; heavy, black bill.
Size: *L* 8–9 in; *W* 13 in.
Voice: loud, whistled *wheep!* and a rolling *prrrrreet!*
Status: common summer resident.
Habitat: deciduous and mixed woodlands and forests, usually near openings or edges.

Similar Birds

Acadian Flycatcher
(p. 96)

Eastern Kingbird
(p. 105)

peaked, "crested" head

reddish brown tail

gray throat and upper breast

bright yellow belly and undertail coverts

Nesting: in a tree cavity or artificial cavity lined with grass; may hang a shed snakeskin over entrance hole; heavily marked, pale buff eggs are $7/8 \times 5/8$ in; female incubates 5 eggs for 13–15 days.

Did You Know?

Many animals depend on tree cavities for shelter and nesting, so instead of cutting down large, dead trees, consider leaving a few standing.

Look For

Follow the loud *wheep!* calls and watch for a show of bright yellow and rufous feathers to find this flycatcher.

Eastern Kingbird
Tyrannus tyrannus

Sometimes referred to as the "Jekyll and Hyde" bird, the Eastern Kingbird is a gregarious fruit eater while wintering in South America, and an antisocial, aggressive insect eater while nesting in North America. • The Eastern Kingbird fearlessly attacks crows, hawks and even humans that pass through its territory, pursuing and pecking at them until the threat has passed. No one familiar with the Eastern Kingbird's pugnacious behavior will refute its scientific name, *Tyrannus tyrannus*. This bird reveals a gentler side of its character in its quivering, butterfly-like courtship flight.

Other ID: black bill and legs; no eye ring; white underparts; grayish breast.
Size: *L* 8½–9 in; *W* 15 in.
Voice: call is a quick, loud, chattering *kit-kit-kitter-kitter;* also a *buzzy dzee-dzee-dzee.*
Status: common summer resident.
Habitat: fields with scattered shrubs, trees or hedgerows, forest fringes, clearings, shrubby roadsides, towns and farmyards.

Similar Birds

Eastern Phoebe
(p. 100)

Look For

Eastern Kingbirds are common and widespread. On a drive in the country you will likely spot at least one of these birds sitting on a fence or utility wire.

thin, orange-red crown (rarely seen)

small head crest

dark gray to black upperparts

white-tipped tail

Nesting: on a horizontal limb, stump or upturned tree root; cup nest is made of weeds, twigs and grass; darkly blotched, white to pinkish white eggs are 1 x ¾ in; female incubates 3–4 eggs for 14–18 days.

Did You Know?

For an Eastern Kingbird, bathing involves repeatedly flying close enough to the surface of the water to wet its head and breast. Then it settles on a perch to preen itself.

Loggerhead Shrike

Lanius ludovicianus

The Loggerhead Shrike is truly in a class of its own. This predatory songbird has very acute vision, and it often perches atop trees and on wires to scan for small prey, which is caught in fast, direct flight or a swooping dive. • Males display their hunting prowess by impaling prey on thorns or barbed wire. This behavior may also serve as a means of storing excess food during times of plenty. • Many shrikes become traffic fatalities when they fly low across roads to prey on insects attracted to the warm pavement.

Other ID: gray crown and back; white underparts.
In flight: white wing patches; white-edged tail.
Size: *L* 9 in; *W* 12 in.
Voice: *Male:* high-pitched, hiccupy *bird-ee bird-ee* in summer; infrequently a harsh *shack-shack* year-round.
Status: declining uncommon to locally rare permanent resident.
Habitat: grazed pastures and marginal and abandoned farmlands with scattered hawthorn shrubs, fence posts, barbed wire and nearby wetlands.

Similar Birds

Northern Mockingbird
(p. 136)

Look For

Shrikes typically perch at the top of tall trees to survey the surrounding area for prey.

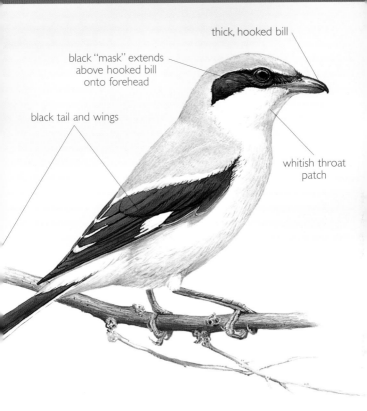

thick, hooked bill

black "mask" extends
above hooked bill
onto forehead

black tail and wings

whitish throat
patch

Nesting: low in a shrub or small tree; bulky cup
nest of twigs and grass is lined with animal hair,
feathers and plant down; darkly blotched, pale
buff to grayish white eggs are 1 x ¾ in; female
incubates 5–6 eggs for 15–17 days.

Did You Know?

Habitat loss has contributed to a steady decline in Loggerhead
Shrike populations, earning this bird endangered species status
in some states. Of the world's 30 shrike species, the Loggerhead
is the only one that occurs exclusively in North America.

White-eyed Vireo
Vireo griseus

Renowned for their complex vocalizations, a single White-eyed Vireo can have a repertoire of a dozen or more songs. This vireo is also an excellent vocal mimic and may incorporate the calls of other bird species in its own songs! • Even more cryptic than the bird itself is the location of its precious nest. Intricately woven from grass, twigs, bark, lichen, moss, plant down, leaves and the fibrous paper from a wasp nest, the nest of the White-eyed Vireo is hung between the forking branches of a tree or shrub.

Other ID: olive gray upperparts; white underparts; 2 whitish wing bars; dark wings and tail.
Size: *L* 5 in; *W* 7½ in.
Voice: loud, snappy, 3–9-note song, usually beginning and ending with *chick*: *chick-ticha-wheeyou, chick-ticha-wheeyou-chick!*
Status: common migrant and summer resident.
Habitat: dense, shrubby undergrowth and thickets in open, swampy, deciduous woodlands, overgrown fields, young second-growth woodlands, woodland clearings and along woodlot edges.

Similar Birds

Red-eyed Vireo

Pine Warbler

Yellow-throated Vireo

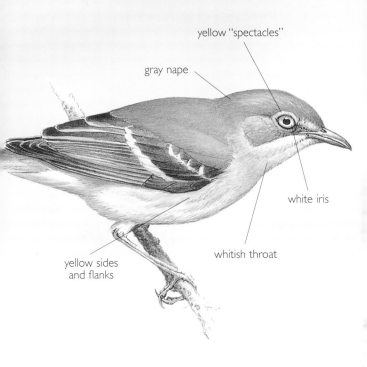

yellow "spectacles"

gray nape

white iris

whitish throat

yellow sides
and flanks

Nesting: in a deciduous shrub or small tree; cup
nest hangs from a horizontal fork; lightly speckled,
white eggs are ¾ x ⁹⁄₁₆ in; pair incubates 4 eggs
for 13–15 days; both adults feed the young.

Did You Know?

When insects are scarce,
White-eyed Vireos will
eat berries, preferably
green briar or honey-
suckle.

Look For

The color of this bird's iris
can help determine age: a
juvenile White-eyed Vireo
has dark eyes that change to
a unique white color as the
bird matures.

Blue Jay

Cyanocitta cristata

The Blue Jay is the only member of the corvid family dressed in blue in Kentucky. White-flecked wing feathers and sharply defined facial features make this bird easy to recognize. • Jays can be quite aggressive when competing for sunflower seeds and peanuts at backyard feeding stations and rarely hesitate to drive away smaller birds, squirrels or even threatening cats. Even the Great Horned Owl is not too formidable a predator for a group of these brave, boisterous mobsters to harass.

Other ID: blue upperparts; white underparts; black bill.

Size: *L* 11–12 in; *W* 16 in.

Voice: noisy, screaming *jay-jay-jay;* nasal *queedle queedle queedle-queedle* sounds like a muted trumpet; often imitates various sounds, including calls of other birds.

Status: common permanent resident.

Habitat: mixed deciduous forests, agricultural areas, scrubby fields and townsites.

Similar Birds

Belted Kingfisher
(p. 84)

Eastern Bluebird
(p. 128)

Blue Grosbeak
(p. 164)

blue crest

black "necklace"

white bar and flecking
on the wings

dark bars and
white corners
on blue tail

Nesting: in a tree or tall shrub; pair builds
a bulky stick nest; greenish, buff or pale eggs,
spotted with gray and brown, are 1⅛ x ¾ in;
pair incubates 4–5 eggs for 16–18 days.

Did You Know?

Blue Jays store food from
feeders in trees and
other places for later use.

Look For

What may appear to be
a dozen or so regulars at a
feeder are often actually
three or four individuals
"making the rounds."

American Crow
Corvus brachyrhynchos

The noise that most often emanates from this treetop squawker seems unrepresentative of its intelligence. However, this wary, clever bird is also an impressive mimic, able to whine like a dog and laugh or cry like a human. • American Crows have flourished in spite of considerable efforts, over many generations, to reduce their numbers. As ecological generalists, crows can survive in a wide variety of habitats and conditions. In January, when crows in Kentucky are busy capturing frogs and lizards in thriving wetlands, crows in more northerly locales are searching snow-covered fields for mice or carrion.

Other ID: glossy, purple-black plumage; black bill and legs.
Size: *L* 17–21 in; W 3 ft.
Voice: distinctive, far-carrying, repetitive *caw-caw-caw*.
Status: common permanent resident.
Habitat: urban areas, agricultural fields and other open areas with scattered woodlands.

Similar Birds

Fish Crow

Common Grackle
(p. 172)

Common Raven

slim, sleek head
and throat

square-shaped
tail

Nesting: in a tree or on a utility pole; large stick-and-branch nest is lined with fur and soft plant material; darkly blotched, gray-green to blue-green eggs are 1⅝ x 1⅛ in; female incubates 4–6 eggs for about 18 days.

Did You Know?

Crows are family oriented, and the young from the previous year may help their parents to raise the nestlings.

Look For

The American Crow has a square tail and a slimmer bill than the larger but similar-looking Common Raven.

Purple Martin
Progne subis

These large swallows will entertain you throughout spring and summer in return for you setting up luxurious "condo complexes" for them. You can watch martin adults spiral around their accommodations in pursuit of flying insects, while their young perch clumsily at the cavity openings. Purple Martins once nested in natural tree hollows and in cliff crevices but now have virtually abandoned these in favor of human-made housing. • To avoid the invasion of aggressive House Sparrows or European Starlings, it is essential for martin condos to be cleaned out and closed up after each nesting season.

Other ID: pointed wings; small bill.
Size: *L* 7–8 in; *W* 18 in.
Voice: rich, fluty, robinlike *pew-pew*, often heard in flight.
Status: fairly common summer resident.
Habitat: semi-open areas, often near water.

Similar Birds

European Starling
(p. 140)

Northern Rough-winged
Swallow (p. 116)

Bank Swallow

sooty gray underparts on female

glossy, dark blue body

slightly forked tail

♀

♂

dark underparts on male

slightly forked tail

Nesting: communal; in a birdhouse or a hollowed-out gourd; nest is made of feathers, grass and mud; white eggs are 1 x ⅝ in; female incubates 4–5 eggs for 15–18 days.

Did You Know?

The Purple Martin is North America's largest swallow.

Look For

You will have better success attracting Purple Martins to your martin condo complex if it is erected in an open area, high on a pole and near a body of water.

Northern Rough-winged Swallow

Stelgidopteryx serripennis

Northern Rough-winged Swallows are more widespread in Kentucky than most people realize. They typically nest in sandy banks along rivers and streams, but vertical cuts created by interstate highways have provided additional nesting crevices for these dusky little birds. Watch for Rough-wings zipping through busy intersections near banks, culverts and bridges. • Male Northern Rough-wings have unique, curved barbs along the outer edge of their primary wing feathers. The purpose of this saw-toothed edge remains a mystery, but it may be used to produce sound during courtship displays.

Other ID: small bill; dark rump; plumage color varies considerably in populations. *In flight:* notched tail.
Size: L 5½ in; W 14 in.
Voice: generally quiet; occasionally a quick, short, squeaky *brrrtt*.
Status: common summer resident.
Habitat: open and semi-open areas, including fields and open woodlands, usually near water; also gravel pits.

Similar Birds

Bank Swallow

Tree Swallow

Purple Martin
(p. 114)

dark "cheek"

drab brown overall

long, pointed
wings

gray-brown throat,
chest and sides

Nesting: occasionally in a small colony; pair
excavates a long burrow in a steep earthen bank;
may use an existing burrow; nest is lined with
leaves; white eggs are ⅝ x ½ in; mostly the
female incubates 4–8 eggs for 12–16 days.

Did You Know?

This bird drinks while flying by dipping its bill into
the water.

Look For

The Rough-wing is more
likely than other swallows to
feed over water, picking off
insects on or near the
water's surface.

Barn Swallow
Hirundo rustica

When you encounter this bird, you might first notice its distinctive, deeply forked tail—or you might just find yourself repeatedly ducking to avoid the dives of a protective parent. Barn Swallows once nested on cliffs, but they are now found more frequently nesting on barns, boat-houses and under bridges and house eaves. The messy young and aggressive parents unfortunately often motivate people to remove nests just as nesting season is beginning, but this bird's close association with humans allows us to observe the normally secretive reproductive cycle of birds.

Other ID: blue-black upperparts; long, pointed wings.
Size: *L* 7 in; *W* 15 in.
Voice: continuous, twittering chatter: *zip-zip-zip* or *kvick-kvick.*
Status: common summer resident.
Habitat: open rural and urban areas where bridges, culverts and build- ings are found near water.

Similar Birds

Cliff Swallow

Bank Swallow

rufous throat and forehead

black "necklace"

rust- to buff-colored underparts

long, deeply forked tail

Nesting: singly or in a small, loose colony; on a human-made structure under an overhang; half or full cup nest is made of mud, grass and straw; brown-spotted, white eggs are ¾ x ½ in; pair incubates 4–7 eggs for 13–17 days.

Did You Know?

The Barn Swallow is a natural pest controller, feeding on insects that are often harmful to crops and livestock.

Look For

Barn Swallows roll mud into small balls and build their nests one mouthful of mud at a time.

Carolina Chickadee
Poecile carolinensis

Fidgety, friendly Carolina Chickadees are familiar to anyone with a backyard feeder well stocked with sunflower seeds and peanut butter. These agile birds even hang upside down to pluck up insects and berries. Like some woodpeckers and nuthatches, the Carolina Chickadee will hoard food for later in the season when food may become scarce. • It's hard to imagine a chickadee using its tiny bill to excavate a nesting cavity, but come breeding season, this ener-getic little bird can be found hammering out a hol-low in a rotting tree. • Where the ranges of the Carolina Chickadee and the Black-capped Chickadee (*P. atricapillus*) overlap in the Appalachians, the Carolina Chickadee tends to stick to lower elevations.

Other ID: white "cheek"; white underparts.
Size: L 4¾ in; W 7½ in.
Voice: whistling song has 4 clear notes: *fee-bee fee-bay.*
Status: common permanent resident.
Habitat: deciduous and mixed woods, riparian woodlands, groves and isolated shade trees; frequents urban areas.

Similar Birds

Black-capped
Chickadee

White-breasted
Nuthatch

Blackpoll Warbler

black cap and "bib"

grayish nape

gray upperparts
and secondaries

buffy flanks

Nesting: excavates or enlarges a tree cavity; may
use a nest box; cavity is lined with feathers, hair
and plant fibers; brown-marked, white eggs are $\frac{9}{16}$
x $\frac{7}{16}$ in; female incubates 5–8 eggs for 11–14 days.

Did You Know?

Each fall, adult Carolina
Chickadees tour the
neighborhood, introducing
their offspring to the best
feeding spots.

Look For

Alert Carolina Chickadees
are often the first to issue
alarm calls, warning other
birds that danger is near.

Tufted Titmouse
Baeolophus bicolor

This bird's amusing feeding antics and insatiable appetite keep curious observers entertained at bird feeders. Grasping a sunflower seed with its tiny feet, the dexterous Tufted Titmouse will strike its dainty bill repeatedly against the hard outer coating to expose the inner core. • A breeding pair of Tufted Titmice will maintain their bond throughout the year, even when joining small, mixed flocks for the cold winter months. The titmouse family bond is so strong that the young from one breeding season will often stay with their parents long enough to help them with nesting and feeding duties the following year.

Other ID: white underparts; pale face.
Size: L 6–6½ in; W 10 in.
Voice: noisy, scolding call; song is a whistled *peter peter* or *peter peter peter*.
Status: common permanent resident.
Habitat: deciduous woodlands, groves and suburban parks with large, mature trees.

Look For

Easily identified by its gray crest and upperparts and black forehead, the Tufted Titmouse can often be seen at feeders. Studies have shown that titmice always choose the largest sunflower seeds available to them, and during winter, they often cache food in bark crevices.

gray crest

black forehead

gray upperparts

buffy flanks

Nesting: in a natural cavity or an abandoned woodpecker nest; cavity is lined with soft vegetation, moss and animal hair; brown-speckled, white eggs are $^{11}/_{16}$ x $^{9}/_{16}$ in; female incubates 5–6 eggs for 12–14 days.

Did You Know?

Nesting pairs search for soft nest lining material in late winter and may accept an offering of the hair that has accumulated in your hairbrush.

White-breasted Nuthatch
Sitta carolinensis

Its upside-down antics and noisy, nasal call make the White-breasted Nuthatch a favorite among novice birders. Whether you spot this black-capped bullet spiraling headfirst down a tree or clinging to the underside of a branch in search of invertebrates, the nuthatch's odd behavior deserves a second glance.

• Comparing the White-breasted Nuthatch to the Carolina Chickadee, both regular visitors to backyard feeders, is a perfect starting point for introductory birding. While both have dark crowns and gray backs, the nuthatch's foraging behavior and undulating flight pattern are distinctive.

Other ID: white underparts and face; straight bill; short legs. *Male:* black cap. *Female:* dark gray cap.
Size: L 5½–6 in; W 11 in.
Voice: song is a fast, nasal *yank-hank yank-hank*, lower than the Red-breasted Nuthatch; calls include *ha-ha-ha ha-ha-ha, ank ank* and *ip*.
Status: fairly common permanent resident.
Habitat: mixedwood forests, woodlots and backyards.

Similar Birds

Red-breasted Nuthatch

Carolina Chickadee
(p. 120)

Brown Creeper

rusty undertail coverts

short tail

gray blue back

dark crown

Nesting: in a natural cavity or an abandoned woodpecker nest; female lines the cavity with soft material; brown-speckled, white eggs are ¾ x ⁹⁄₁₆ in; female incubates 5–8 eggs for 12–14 days.

Did You Know?

Nuthatches are presumably named for their habit of wedging seeds and nuts into crevices and hacking them open with their bills.

Look For

Nuthatches grasp trees through foot power alone, unlike woodpeckers, which use their tails to brace themselves against tree trunks.

Carolina Wren
Thryothorus ludovicianus

The energetic and cheerful Carolina Wren can be shy and retiring, often hiding deep inside dense shrubbery. The best opportunity for viewing this particularly vocal wren is when it sits on a conspicuous perch while unleashing its impressive song. Pairs perform lively "duets" at any time of day and in any season. The duet often begins with introductory chatter by the female, followed by innumerable ringing variations of *tea-kettle tea-kettle tea-kettle tea* from her mate. • Carolina Wrens readily nest in the brushy thickets of an overgrown backyard or in an obscure nook or crevice in a house or barn. If conditions are favorable, two broods may be raised in a single season.

Other ID: white throat; slightly downcurved bill.
Size: L 5½ in; W 7½ in.
Voice: loud, repetitious *tea-kettle tea-kettle tea-kettle* may be heard at any time of day or year; female often chatters while male sings.
Status: common permanent resident.
Habitat: dense forest undergrowth, especially shrubby tangles and thickets.

Similar Birds

House Wren

Red-breasted Nuthatch

long, prominent, white "eyebrow"

rusty brown upperparts

rich buff-colored underparts

Nesting: in a nest box or natural or artificial cavity; nest is lined with soft material and may include a snakeskin; brown-blotched, white eggs are ¾ x ⁹⁄₁₆ in; female incubates 4–5 eggs for 12–16 days.

Did You Know?

In mild winters, Carolina Wren populations remain stable, but frigid temperatures can temporarily decimate an otherwise healthy population.

Look For

Carolina Wrens sometimes nest in hanging flowerpots or in abandoned buildings.

Eastern Bluebird
Sialia sialis

The Eastern Bluebird's enticing colors are like those of a warm setting sun against a deep blue sky. • This cavity nester's survival has been put to the test—populations have declined in the presence of the competitive, introduced House Sparrow and European Starling. The removal of standing dead trees has also diminished nest site availability. Thankfully, bluebird enthusiasts and organizations have developed "bluebird trails" and mounted nest boxes on fence posts along highways and rural roads, allowing Eastern Bluebird numbers to gradually recover.

Other ID: dark bill and legs. *Female:* thin, white eye ring; gray-brown head and back tinged with blue; blue wings and tail; paler chestnut underparts.
Size: *L* 7 in; *W* 13 in.
Voice: song is a rich, warbling *turr, turr-lee, turr-lee;* call is a chittering *pew.*
Status: fairly common permanent resident.
Habitat: fencelines, meadows, fallow fields, forest clearings and edges, golf courses, large lawns and cemeteries.

Similar Birds

Blue Grosbeak
(p. 164)

Indigo Bunting
(p. 166)

deep blue
upperparts

chestnut red
"chin," throat
and sides

white belly and
undertail
coverts

♂

Nesting: in a natural cavity or nest box; female builds a cup nest of grass, weed stems and small twigs; pale blue eggs are $\frac{7}{8}$ x $\frac{5}{8}$ in; female incubates 4–5 eggs for 13–16 days.

Did You Know?

A cold spell in spring can kill the Eastern Bluebird, freezing the eggs and adult while it sits on the nest.

Look For

Bluebirds have straight, pointed bills that are perfect for capturing insects. They also feed on berries and are especially attracted to wild grapes, sumac and currants.

Wood Thrush
Hylocichla mustelina

The loud, warbled notes of the Wood Thrush once resounded through our woodlands, but forest fragmentation and urban sprawl have eliminated much of this bird's nesting habitat. Broken forests and diminutive woodlots have allowed the invasion of common, open-area predators and parasites, such as raccoons, skunks, crows, jays and cowbirds. Traditionally, these predators had little access to nests that were hidden deep within vast hardwood forests. Many forests that have been urbanized or developed for agriculture now host families of American Robins rather than the once-prominent Wood Thrushes.

Other ID: plump body; streaked "cheeks"; brown wings, rump and tail.
Size: *L* 8 in; *W* 13 in.
Voice: *Male:* bell-like phrases of 3–5 notes, with each note at a different pitch and followed by a trill: *Will you live with me? Way up high in a tree, I'll come right down and…seeee!;* calls include a *pit pit* and *bweebeebeep.*
Status: fairly common summer resident.
Habitat: moist, mature and preferably undisturbed deciduous woodlands and mixed forests.

Similar Birds

Hermit Thrush

Swainson's Thrush

Veery

bold, white
eye ring

rusty head
and back

large black spots
on white breast,
sides and flanks

Nesting: low in a deciduous tree; female builds a bulky cup nest of vegetation held together with mud and lined with softer material; pale greenish blue eggs are 1 x ¾ in; female incubates 3–4 eggs for 13–14 days.

Did You Know?

Henry David Thoreau considered the Wood Thrush's song to be the most beautiful of avian sounds. The male can even sing two notes at once!

Look For

Wood Thrushes forage on the ground or glean vegetation for insects and other invertebrates.

American Robin
Turdus migratorius

Come March, the familiar song of the American Robin may wake you early if you are a light sleeper. This abundant bird adapts easily to urban areas and often works from dawn until after dusk when there is a nest to be built or hungry, young mouths to feed. • The robin's bright red belly contrasts with its dark head and wings, making this bird easy to identify. • In winter, fruit trees may attract flocks of robins, which gather to drink the fermenting fruit's intoxicating juices.

Other ID: incomplete, white eye ring; gray-brown back; white undertail coverts.
Size: *L* 10 in; *W* 17 in.
Voice: song is an evenly spaced warble: *cheerily cheer-up cheerio;* call is a rapid *tut-tut-tut.*
Status: common permanent resident.
Habitat: *Breeding:* residential lawns and gardens, pastures, urban parks, broken forests, bogs and river shorelines. *Winter:* near fruit-bearing trees and springs.

Similar Birds

Varied Thrush

Veery

black-tipped, yellow bill

dark gray head

black head

white throat streaked with black

brick red breast is darker on male

Nesting: in a tree or shrub; cup nest is built of grass, moss, bark and mud; light blue eggs are 1⅛ x ¾ in; female incubates 4 eggs for 11–16 days; raises up to 3 broods per year.

Did You Know?

Robins usually raise two broods per year, and the male cares for the fledglings from the first brood while the female incubates the second clutch of eggs.

Look For

A hunting robin with its head tilted to the side isn't listening for prey—it is actually looking for movements in the soil.

Gray Catbird

Dumetella carolinensis

The Gray Catbird is an accomplished mimic that may fool you as it shuffles through underbrush and dense riparian shrubs, calling its catlike *meow*. Its mimicking talents are further enhanced by its ability to sing two notes at once, using each side of its syrinx individually.

• The Gray Catbird will vigilantly defend its territory against sparrows, robins, cowbirds and other intruders. It will destroy the eggs and nestlings of other songbirds and will take on an intense defensive posture if approached, screaming and even attempting to hit an intruder.

Other ID: dark gray overall; black eyes, bill and legs.
Size: L 8½–9 in; W 11 in.
Voice: calls include a catlike *meow* and a harsh *check-check;* song is a variety of warbles, squeaks and mimicked phrases interspersed with a *mew* call.
Status: uncommon summer resident.
Habitat: dense thickets, brambles, shrubby or brushy areas and hedgerows, often near water.

Similar Birds

Northern Mockingbird
(p. 136)

Look For

If you catch a glimpse of this bird during breeding season, watch the male raise his long slender tail into the air to show off his rust-colored undertail coverts.

black cap

long, dark gray
to black tail

chestnut undertail
coverts

Nesting: in a dense shrub or thicket; bulky cup nest is made of twigs, leaves and grass; greenish blue eggs are ⅞ × ⅝ in; female incubates 4 eggs for 12–15 days.

Did You Know?

The watchful female Gray Catbird can recognize a Brown-headed Cowbird egg and will remove it from her nest. The ability to recognize the foreign eggs is learned and only about a dozen species are able to do so.

Northern Mockingbird

Mimus polyglottos

The Northern Mockingbird has an amazing vocal repertoire that includes over 400 different song types, which it belts out incessantly throughout the breeding season, serenading into the night during a full moon. Mockingbirds can imitate almost anything. In some instances, they replicate notes so accurately that even computerized sound analysis is unable to detect the difference between the original source and the mockingbird's imitation.

Other ID: gray upperparts; 2 thin, white wing bars; light gray underparts.
Size: *L* 10 in; *W* 14 in.
Voice: song is a medley of mimicked phrases, often repeated 3–6 times; calls include a harsh *chair* and *chewk*.
Status: common permanent resident.
Habitat: hedges, suburban gardens and orchard margins with an abundance of available fruit; hedgerows of roses are especially important in winter.

Similar Birds

Loggerhead Shrike
(p. 106)

Gray Catbird
(p. 134)

long, dark tail with white outer tail feathers

dark wings

thin, dark eye line

Nesting: in a small shrub or tree; cup nest is built with twigs and lined with grass and leaves; brown-blotched, bluish gray to greenish eggs are 1 x ⅝ in; female incubates 3–4 eggs for 12–13 days.

Did You Know?

The scientific name *polyglottos* is Greek for "many tongues" and refers to this bird's ability to mimic a wide variety of sounds.

Look For

Offerings of suet, raisins and fruit at feeders can lure these and other birds into your yard.

Brown Thrasher
Toxostoma rufum

The Brown Thrasher shares the streaked breast of a thrush and the long tail of a catbird, but it has a temper all its own. Because it nests close to the ground, the Brown Thrasher defends its nest with a vengeance, attacking snakes and other nest robbers sometimes to the point of drawing blood.

• Biologists have estimated that the male Brown Thrasher is capable of producing up to 3000 distinctive song phrases—the most extensive vocal repertoire of any North American bird.

Other ID: reddish brown upperparts; long, rufous tail; orange-yellow eyes.
Size: *L* 11½ in; *W* 13 in.
Voice: sings a large variety of phrases, with each phrase usually repeated twice: *dig-it dig-it, hoe-it hoe-it, pull-it-up pull-it-up;* calls include a loud crackling note, a harsh *shuck,* a soft *churr* or a whistled, 3-note *pit-cher-ee.*
Status: common summer resident; uncommon winter resident.
Habitat: dense shrubs and thickets, overgrown pastures, woodland edges and brushy areas; rarely close to urban areas.

Similar Birds

Hermit Thrush

Wood Thrush
(p. 130)

long, downcurved bill

2 white
wing bars

gray "cheek"

pale underparts with
heavy brown streaking

Nesting: usually in a low shrub; often on the ground; cup nest is made of grass, twigs and leaves; pale blue eggs, dotted with reddish brown, are 1 x ¾ in; pair incubates 4 eggs for 11–14 days.

Did You Know?

Fencing shrubby, wooded areas bordering wetlands and streams can prevent cattle from devastating thrasher nesting habitat.

Look For

You might catch only a flash of rufous as the Brown Thrasher flies from one thicket to another in its shrubby understory habitat.

European Starling
Sturnus vulgaris

The European Starling did not hesitate to make itself known across North America after being released in New York's Central Park in 1890 and 1891. This highly adaptable bird not only took over the nest sites of native cavity nesters, such as Tree Swallows and Red-headed Woodpeckers, but it also learned to mimic the sounds of Killdeers, Red-tailed Hawks, Soras and meadowlarks. • Look for European Starlings in massive evening roosts under bridges or on buildings in late summer and through the winter months.

Other ID: dark eyes; short, squared tail. *Nonbreeding:* feather tips are heavily spotted with white and buff.
Size: *L* 8½ in; W 16 in.
Voice: variety of whistles, squeaks, and gurgles; imitates other birds.
Status: common permanent resident.
Habitat: cities, towns, residential areas, farmyards, woodland fringes and clearings.

Similar Birds

Rusty Blackbird

Brown-headed Cowbird (p. 174)

Brewer's Blackbird

iridescent, purple-black head, neck and breast

glossy, green back with buffy spots

yellow bill

breeding

greenish black underparts

Nesting: in an abandoned woodpecker cavity, natural cavity or nest box; nest is made of grass, twigs and straw; bluish to greenish white eggs are $1\frac{1}{8}$ x $\frac{7}{8}$ in; female incubates 4–6 eggs for 12–14 days.

Did You Know?

Starlings were brought to New York as part of the local Shakespeare society's plan to introduce all the birds mentioned in their favorite author's writings.

Look For

Sometimes confused with a blackbird, the European Starling has a shorter tail and a bright yellow bill.

Cedar Waxwing
Bombycilla cedrorum

With its black "mask" and slick hairdo, the Cedar Waxwing has a heroic look. This bird's splendid personality is reflected in its amusing antics after it gorges on fermented berries and in its gentle courtship dance. To court a mate, the gentlemanly male hops toward a female and offers her a berry. The female accepts the berry and hops away, then stops and hops back toward the male to offer him the berry in return. • If a bird's crop is full and it is unable to eat any more, it will continue to pluck fruit and pass it down the line like a bucket brigade, until the fruit is gulped down by a still-hungry bird.

Other ID: brown upperparts; yellow terminal tail band.
Size: *L* 7 in; *W* 12 in.
Voice: faint, high-pitched, trilled whistle: *tseee-tseee-tseee.*
Status: fairly common permanent resident locally; more common in migration.
Habitat: wooded residential parks and gardens, overgrown fields, forest edges, second-growth, riparian and open woodlands; often near fruit trees and water.

Look For

The yellow tail band and "waxy" red wing tips of the Cedar Waxwing get their color from pigments in the berries that these birds eat.

cinnamon crest

black "mask"

small red "drops"
on wings

yellow wash
on belly

white undertail
coverts

Nesting: in a tree or shrub; cup nest is made of twigs, moss and lichen; darkly spotted, bluish to gray eggs are 7/8 x 5/8 in; female incubates 3–5 eggs for 12–16 days.

Did You Know?

Cedar waxwings prefer sugary fruits, which often ferment after ripening. Waxwings will show definite signs of tipsiness after consuming fermented fruit.

Ovenbird
Seiurus aurocapilla

Even the sharpest human eye will have trouble spotting the Ovenbird's immaculately concealed nest along hiking trails and bike paths. An incubating female is usually confident enough in the camouflage of her ground nest that she will choose to sit tight rather than flee in the presence of danger. Furthermore, some females have as many as three mates to call on for protection and to help feed the young. Despite these evolutionary adaptations, forest fragmentation and Brown-headed Cowbird parasitism have reduced this bird's nesting success.

Other ID: olive brown upperparts; no wing bars; white undertail coverts; pink legs.
Size: *L* 6 in; *W* 9½ in.
Voice: loud, distinctive *tea-cher tea-cher tea-CHER tea-CHER,* increasing in speed and volume; night song is a set of bubbly, warbled notes, often ending in *teacher-teacher;* call is a brisk *chip, cheep* or *chock.*
Status: common migrant and summer resident in eastern Kentucky; uncommon elsewhere.
Habitat: *Breeding:* undisturbed, mature forests with a closed canopy and little understory. *In migration:* dense riparian shrubs and thickets.

Similar Birds

Louisiana Waterthrush

Wood Thrush (p. 130)

Hermit Thrush

rufous crown
bordered by black

white eye ring

heavy, dark streaking
on white breast,
sides and flanks

Nesting: on the ground; female builds a domed, oven-shaped nest of grass, twigs, bark and dead leaves, lined with animal hair; white eggs, spotted with gray and brown, are ¾ x ½ in; female incubates 4–5 eggs for 11–13 days.

Did You Know?

The name "Ovenbird" refers to this bird's unusual dome-shaped ground nest.

Look For

In summer, the male's loud *tea-cher* song will give away his presence as he hides among tangled shrubs or conifer branches.

Common Yellowthroat

Geothlypis trichas

The bumblebee colors of the male Common Yellowthroat's black "mask" and yellow throat identify this skulking wetland resident. He sings his *witchety* song from strategically chosen cattail perches that he visits in rotation, fiercely guarding his territory against the intrusion of other males.
• The Common Yellowthroat is different from most wood-warblers, preferring marshlands and wet, overgrown meadows to forests. The female wears no "mask" and remains mostly hidden from view in thick vegetation when she tends to the nest.

Other ID: black bill; orangy legs. *Female:* may show faint, white eye ring.
Size: *L* 5 in; *W* 7 in.
Voice: song is a clear, oscillating *witchety witchety witchety-witch;* call is a sharp *tcheck* or *tchet.*
Status: common summer resident.
Habitat: wetlands, riparian areas and wet, overgrown meadows; sometimes dry fields.

Similar Birds

Wilson's Warbler

Nashville Warbler

Kentucky Warbler
(p. 148)

olive green to olive brown upperparts

yellow throat, breast and undertail coverts

broad, black "mask" with white upper border

dingy white belly

Nesting: on or near the ground; often in a small shrub or emergent vegetation; female builds an open cup nest of weeds, grass, bark strips and moss; brown-blotched, white eggs are ⅝ x ½ in; female incubates 3–5 eggs for 12 days.

Did You Know?

Famous Swedish biologist Carl Linnaeus named the Common Yellowthroat in 1766, making it one of the first North American birds to be described.

Look For

Common Yellowthroats immerse themselves or roll in water, then shake off the excess water by flicking or flapping their wings.

Kentucky Warbler

Oporornis formosus

Kentucky Warblers spend much of their time on the ground, overturning leaves and scurrying through dense thickets in search of insects. These birds are shy and elusive as they sing their loud springtime song from secluded perches. As a general rule, male warblers sing most actively in the morning, feeding only intermittently but quiet down in the afternoon and feed more actively. Once the young hatch, singing becomes rare as both the male and the female spend much of their time feeding the young. Unmated males, however, may continue to sing throughout the summer.

Other ID: olive green upperparts; female has less distinct facial markings.
Size: *L* 5–5½ in; *W* 8½ in.
Voice: musical song is a series of 2-syllable notes: *chur-ree chur-ree* (similar to the song of the Carolina Wren); call is a sharp *chick*.
Status: common migrant and summer resident.
Habitat: moist deciduous and mixed woodlands with dense, shrubby cover and herbaceous plant growth, including wooded ravines, swamp edges and creek bottomlands.

Similar Birds

Canada Warbler

Yellow-throated Warbler

Hooded Warbler

black crown, "sideburns" and "half mask"

bright yellow "spectacles"

bright yellow underparts

Nesting: on or close to the ground; pair builds a cup nest of plant material and hair and lines it with rootlets and hair; brown-blotched, cream-colored eggs are $3/4$ x $9/16$ in; female incubates 4–5 eggs for 12–13 days.

Did You Know?

This warbler's song is similar to the Carolina Wren's, but the warbler sings the same song pattern repeatedly, while the wren constantly varies its song.

Look For

Like waterthrushes and Ovenbirds, Kentucky Warblers bob their tails up and down as they walk.

Yellow-breasted Chat
Icteria virens

Nearly eight inches in length, the Yellow-breasted Chat is quite literally a "warbler and a half." This bird is a member of the wood-warbler clan, and its bright yellow coloration and intense curiosity are typical warbler traits. However, the chat's large size, curious vocalizations and noisy thrashing behavior suggest a closer relationship to the mimic thrushes.
• When much of eastern North America was logged in the early 1900s, the Yellow-breasted Chat became one of our most common breeding birds. Populations have since declined as woodlands have matured and shrubby riparian habitat has been lost to development.

Other ID: white jaw line; heavy, black bill; olive green upperparts; gray-black legs. *Female:* gray lores.
Size: L 7½ in; W 9¾ in.
Voice: single notes or phrases of slurred piping whistles, *kuks*, harsh rattles and "laughs."
Status: common summer resident.
Habitat: dense riparian thickets bordering streams, small ponds and swampy ground; may breed in extensive hillside bramble patches.

Look For

Often heard but difficult to see, this elusive bird avoids detection by skulking through brushy riparian thickets and tangled fencerows. The male is most vocal early in the breeding season.

white "spectacles"

black lores

♂

yellow breast

white undertail coverts

long tail

Nesting: low in a shrub or small tree; well-concealed, bulky nest is made of leaves, straw and weeds, with a tight inner cup woven with bark and plant fibers; darkly spotted, creamy white eggs are ⅞ x ⅝ in; female incubates 3–4 eggs for about 11 days.

Did You Know?

Yellow-breasted Chats are well known for singing at night during spring. Only the males sing, and they have a varied repertoire that may include more than 60 song types.

Scarlet Tanager
Piranga olivacea

The vibrant red of a breeding male Scarlet Tanager may catch your eye in Kentucky's wooded ravines and migrant stopover sites. Because this tanager is more likely to reside in forest canopies, birders tend to hear the Scarlet Tanager before they see it. Its song, a sort of slurred version of the American Robin's, is a much-anticipated sound that announces the arrival of this colorful long-distance migrant. The Scarlet Tanager has the northernmost breeding grounds and longest migration route of all tanager species and is one of two tanager species that routinely nest in Kentucky. • Look for this bird at Land Between the Lakes and on the Cumberland Plateau.

Other ID: *Female:* yellow underparts; yellow eye ring.
Size: *L* 7 in; *W* 11½ in.
Voice: song is a series of 4–5 sweet, clear, whistled phrases; call is *chip-burrr* or *chip-churrr*.
Status: fairly common summer resident.
Habitat: fairly mature, upland deciduous and mixed forests.

Similar Birds

Summer Tanager

Northern Cardinal
(p. 162)

pale bill

olive upperparts

bright red body

♀

gray-brown wings

pure black wings and tail

♂

breeding

Nesting: high in a deciduous tree; female builds a flimsy, shallow cup nest of grass, weeds and twigs; brown-spotted, pale blue green eggs are ⅞ x ⅝ in; female incubates 2–5 eggs for 12–14 days.

Did You Know?

In Central and South America, there are over 200 tanager species in every color imaginable.

Look For

Scarlet Tanagers forage in the forest understory in cold, rainy weather, making them easier to observe.

Eastern Towhee
Pipilo erythrophthalmus

Eastern Towhees are large, colorful members of the sparrow family. These noisy birds are often heard before they are seen as they rustle about in dense undergrowth, craftily scraping back layers of dry leaves to expose the seeds, berries or insects hidden beneath. They employ an unusual two-footed technique to uncover food items—a strategy that is especially important in winter when virtually all of their food is taken from the ground.
• The Eastern Towhee and its western relative, the Spotted Towhee *(P. maculata)*, were once grouped together as the "Rufous-sided Towhee."

Other ID: white outer tail corners; white lower breast and belly; buff undertail coverts; eyes commonly red, but in southeastern U.S. may be white or orange.
Size: L 7–8½ in; W 10½ in.
Voice: song is 2 high, whistled notes followed by a trill: *drink your teeeee*; call is a scratchy, slurred *che-weee!* or *chewink!*
Status: common permanent resident.
Habitat: along woodland edges; in shrubby, abandoned fields and residential areas.

Similar Birds

Dark-eyed Junco
(p. 160)

Look For

Showy towhees are easily attracted to feeders, where they scratch on the ground for millet, oats or sunflower seeds.

black back, "hood" and bill

brown "hood" and upperparts

small, white wing patch

♂

rufous sides and flanks

♀

Nesting: on the ground or low in a dense shrub; female builds a cup nest of twigs, bark strips, grass and animal hair; pale, brown-spotted eggs are $7/8$ x $5/8$ in; mainly the female incubates 3–4 eggs for 12–13 days.

Did You Know?

The scientific name *erythrophthalmus* means "red eye" in Greek, though towhees in the southeastern states may have white or orange irises.

Field Sparrow
Spizella pusilla

A plaintive whistle issued from an overgrown field, pasture or forest clearing can alert birders to the Field Sparrow's presence. This gentle bird breeds throughout our state, concealing a delicate nest near the ground, among bushes or in clumps of tall grass. • Over time the Field Sparrow has learned to recognize when its nest has been parasitized by the Brown-headed Cowbird. Since the unwelcome eggs are usually too large for this small sparrow to eject, the nest is simply abandoned. Field Sparrows may make numerous nesting attempts in a single season.

Other ID: gray face and throat; 2 white wing bars; pinkish legs. *Rufous morph:* rusty streak behind eye; buffy red wash on breast, sides and flanks.
Size: L 5–6 in; W 8 in.
Voice: song is a series of woeful, musical, down-slurred whistles accelerating into a trill; call is a *chip* or *tsee*.
Status: common permanent resident.
Habitat: abandoned or weedy and overgrown fields and pastures, woodland edges and clearings, extensive shrubby riparian areas and young conifer plantations.

Similar Birds

Chipping Sparrow

American Tree Sparrow

rusty crown with
gray central stripe

large
orange-pink bill

breeding

white eye
ring

long tail

unmarked, gray or
buffy underparts

Nesting: on or near the ground, often sheltered by a shrub; female weaves an open cup nest of grass and lines it with soft material; brown-spotted, whitish to pale bluish eggs are $5/8$ x $1/2$ in; female incubates 3–5 eggs for 10–12 days.

Did You Know?

In fall, hundreds of Field Sparrows may crowd into weedy fields to feed.

Look For

Its pink bill and rusty crown can help to distinguish the Field Sparrow from similar small brown birds.

White-throated Sparrow

Zonotrichia albicollis

The White-throated Sparrow's distinctive song makes it one of the easiest sparrows to learn and identify. Its familiar bold, white throat and striped crown can only be confused with the White-crowned Sparrow *(Z. leucophrys)*, but White-throats usually stick to forested woodlands, whereas White-crowns prefer open, bushy habitats and farmlands. • Two color morphs are common: one has black and white stripes on the head; the other has brown and tan stripes. These two color morphs are perpetuated because each morph almost always breeds with the opposite color morph.

Other ID: gray "cheek"; black eye line; unstreaked, gray underparts; mottled brown upperparts.
Size: *L* 6½–7½ in; *W* 9 in.
Voice: variable song is a clear, distinct, whistled: *Old Sam Peabody, Peabody, Peabody;* call is a sharp *chink.*
Status: common winter resident.
Habitat: woodlots, wooded parks and riparian brush.

Similar Birds

White-crowned Sparrow

Swamp Sparrow

black and white
(or brown and tan)
striped head

yellow lores

white throat

grayish bill

*white-striped
morph*

Nesting: does not nest in Kentucky; nests in the northeastern U.S. and Canada; on or near the ground, often concealed by a low shrub or fallen log; open cup nest of plant material is lined with fine grass and hair; variably marked, bluish eggs are $7/8$ x $9/16$ in; female incubates 4–5 eggs for 11–14 days.

Did You Know?

Zonotrichia means "hair-like," a reference to the striped heads of birds in this genus.

Look For

Urban backyards dressed with brushy fenceline tangles and a bird feeder brimming with seeds can attract good numbers of these delightful sparrows.

Dark-eyed Junco

Junco hyemalis

Juncos usually congregate in backyards with bird feeders and sheltering conifers—with such amenities at their disposal, more and more juncos are appearing in urban areas. These birds spend most of their time on the ground, snatching up seeds underneath bird feeders, and they are readily flushed from wooded trails and backyard feeders. Their distinctive, white outer tail feathers flash in alarm as they seek cover in a nearby tree or shrub.
• The junco is often called the "Snow Bird," and the species name, *hyemalis*, means "winter" in Greek.
• Look for juncos on Black Mountain in Harlan County in summer and at backyard feeders in winter.

Other ID: *Female:* gray-brown where male is slate gray.
Size: *L* 6–7 in; *W* 9 in.
Voice: song is a long, dry trill; call is a smacking *chip* note, often given in series.
Status: common winter resident throughout the state.
Habitat: shrubby woodland borders, backyard feeders.

Similar Birds

Eastern Towhee
(p. 154)

Look For

This bird will flash its distinctive white outer tail feathers as it rushes for cover after being flushed.

pale pink bill

dark slate gray
overall

white outer tail
feathers

white belly and
undertail coverts

♂

"Slate-colored Junco"

Nesting: on the ground, usually concealed; female
builds a cup nest of twigs, grass, bark shreds and
moss; brown-marked, whitish to bluish eggs are
¾ x ½ in; female incubates 3–5 eggs for 12–13 days.

Did You Know?

There are five closely related Dark-eyed Junco subspecies
in North America that share similar habits but differ in coloration and range.

Northern Cardinal
Cardinalis cardinalis

This colorful, year-round resident is Kentucky's state bird. • A male Northern Cardinal will display his unforgettable, vibrant red head crest and raise his tail when he is excited or agitated. The male will vigorously defend his territory, even attacking his own reflection in a window or hubcap!
• Cardinals are one of only a few bird species to maintain strong pair bonds. Some couples sing to each other year-round, while others join loose flocks, reestablishing pair bonds in spring during a "courtship feeding." A male offers a seed to the female, which she then accepts and eats.

Other ID: *Male:* red overall. *Female:* brownish buff overall; fainter "mask"; red crest, wings and tail.
Size: *L* 8–9 in; *W* 12 in.
Voice: call is a metallic *chip*; song is series of clear, bubbly whistled notes: *What cheer! What cheer! birdie-birdie-birdie what cheer!*
Status: common permanent resident.
Habitat: brushy thickets and shrubby tangles along forest and woodland edges; backyards and urban and suburban parks.

Similar Birds

Summer Tanager

Scarlet Tanager
(p. 152)

pointed crest

red, conical bill

black "mask" and throat

♀

♂

Nesting: in a dense shrub or vine tangle or low in a coniferous tree; female builds an open cup nest of twigs, grass and bark shreds; brown-speckled, white to greenish eggs are 1 x ¾ in; female incubates 3–4 eggs for 12–13 days.

Did You Know?

This bird owes its name to the vivid red plumage of the male, which resembles the robes of Roman Catholic cardinals.

Look For

Northern Cardinals fly with jerky movements and short glides and have a preference for sunflower seeds.

Blue Grosbeak
Passerina caerulea

Male Blue Grosbeaks owe their spectacular spring plumage not to a fresh molt but, oddly enough, to feather wear. While Blue Grosbeaks are wintering in Mexico or Central America, their brown feather tips slowly wear away, leaving the crystal blue plumage that is seen as they arrive on their breeding grounds. The lovely blue color of the plumage is not produced by pigmentation, but by tiny particles in the feathers that reflect only short wavelengths in the light spectrum. • In spring, watch for the tail-spreading, tail-flicking and crown-raising behaviors that suggest the birds might be breeding.

Other ID: *Male:* black around base of bill. *Female:* whitish throat; rump and shoulders are faintly washed with blue.
Size: L 6–7½ in; W 11 in.
Voice: sweet, melodious, warbling song with phrases that rise and fall; call is a loud *chink*.
Status: fairly common migrant and summer resident.
Habitat: thick brush, riparian thickets, shrubby areas and dense weedy fields near water.

Similar Birds

Indigo Bunting
(p. 166)

Look For

A pair of rusty wing bars, visible even on first-winter birds, distinguish the Blue Grosbeak from the similar but more common Indigo Bunting.

blue overall

2 rusty
wing bars

stubby, pale grayish
conical bill

♂

long tail

♀

soft brown
plumage overall

Nesting: in a shrub or low tree; cup nest is
woven with twigs, roots and grass and lined with
finer material, including paper and occasionally
shed reptile skins; pale blue eggs are ⅞ x ⅝ in;
female incubates 2–5 eggs for 11–12 days.

Did You Know?

Caerulea is from the Latin for "blue," a description that just
doesn't express this bird's true beauty. At a distance, the
male's striking blue plumage may look blackish.

Indigo Bunting
Passerina cyanea

The vivid electric blue male Indigo Bunting is one of the most spectacular birds in Kentucky. These birds arrive in April or May and favor raspberry thickets as nest sites. Dense, thorny stems keep most predators at a distance and the berries are a good food source. • The male is a persistent singer, vocalizing even through the heat of a summer day. A young male doesn't learn his couplet song from his parents, but from neighboring males during his first year on his own. • Planting coneflowers, cosmos or foxtail grasses may attract Indigo Buntings to your backyard.

Other ID: beady, black eyes; black legs; no wing bars. *Male:* bright blue overall; black lores. *Female:* soft brown overall; whitish throat.
Size: L 5½ in; W 8 in.
Voice: song consists of paired warbled whistles: *fire-fire, where-where, here-here, see-it see-it;* call is a quick *spit.*
Status: abundant migrant and summer resident.
Habitat: deciduous forest and woodland edges, regenerating forest clearings, orchards and shrubby fields.

Similar Birds

Blue Grosbeak
(p. 164)

Eastern Bluebird
(p. 128)

darker blue head

gray, conical bill

♂

faint brown
streaks on breast

♀

wings and tail may
show some black

breeding

Nesting: in a small tree, shrub or within a vine
tangle; female builds a cup nest of grass, leaves
and bark strips; unmarked, white to bluish white
eggs are ¾ x ½ in; female incubates 3–4 eggs for
12–13 days.

Did You Know?

Females choose the most
melodious males as
mates, because these
males can usually estab-
lish territories with the
finest habitat.

Look For

The Indigo Bunting will land
midway on a stem of grass
or a weed and shuffle slowly
toward the seed head, bend-
ing down the stem to reach
the seeds.

Red-winged Blackbird

Agelaius phoeniceus

The male Red-winged Blackbird wears his bright red shoulders like armor—together with his short, raspy song, they are key in defending his territory from rivals. In field experiments, males whose red shoulders were painted black soon lost their territories. • Nearly every cattail marsh worthy of note in Kentucky hosts Red-winged Blackbirds during at least some of the year. • The female's cryptic coloration allows her to sit inconspicuously on her nest, blending in perfectly with the surroundings.

Other ID: *Male:* black overall. *Female:* mottled brown upperparts; pale "eyebrow."
Size: *L* 7½–9 in; *W* 13 in.
Voice: song is a loud, raspy *konk-a-ree* or *ogle-reeeee;* calls include a harsh *check* and high *tseert;* female gives a loud *che-che-che chee chee chee.*
Status: common permanent resident.
Habitat: cattail marshes, wet meadows and ditches, croplands and shoreline shrubs.

Similar Birds

Brewer's Blackbird

Rusty Blackbird

Brown-headed Cowbird (p. 174)

red shoulder patch
edged in yellow

♂

♀

faint, red
shoulder patch

heavily streaked
underparts

Nesting: colonial; in cattails or shoreline bushes; female builds an open cup nest of dried cattail leaves lined with fine grass; darkly marked, pale bluish green eggs are 1 x ¾ in; female incubates 3–4 eggs for 10–12 days.

Did You Know?

Some scientists believe that the Red-winged Blackbird is the most abundant bird species in North America.

Look For

Red-winged Blackbirds gather in immense flocks in agricultural areas and open fields in winter.

Eastern Meadowlark
Sturnella magna

The drab dress of most female songbirds lends them protection during the breeding season, but the female Eastern Meadowlark uses a different strategy. Her V-shaped "necklace" and bright yellow throat and belly create a colorful distraction that leads predators away from the nest. A female flushed from the nest while incubating her eggs will often abandon the nest, and though she will never abandon her chicks, her extra vigilance following a threat usually results in less frequent feeding of nestlings.

Other ID: yellow underparts; mottled brown upperparts; long, sharp bill; blackish crown stripes and eye line; pale "eyebrow" and median crown stripe; long, pinkish legs.
Size: *L* 9–9½ in; *W* 14 in.
Voice: song is a rich series of 2–8 melodic, clear, slurred whistles: *see-you at school-today* or *this is the year;* gives a rattling flight call and a high, buzzy *dzeart.*
Status: common permanent resident.
Habitat: grassy meadows and pastures, some croplands, weedy fields, grassy roadsides and old orchards.

Similar Birds

Western Meadowlark

Dickcissel

yellow lores

short, wide tail with
white outer tail feathers

white
jaw line

broad, black
breast band

dark streaking
on white sides
and flanks

breeding

Nesting: in a concealed depression on the
ground; female builds a domed grass nest, woven
into surrounding vegetation; heavily spotted, white
eggs are 1⅛ x ¾ in; female incubates 3–7 eggs for
13–15 days.

Did You Know?

Although the name sug-
gests that this bird is a
lark, it is actually a brightly
colored member of the
blackbird family.

Look For

The Eastern Meadowlark
often whistles its proud song
from fence posts and power
lines. Song is the best way to
tell it apart from the very
rare Western Meadowlark.

Common Grackle
Quiscalus quiscula

The Common Grackle is a poor but spirited singer. Usually while perched in a shrub, a male grackle will slowly take a deep breath to inflate his breast, causing his feathers to spike outward, then close his eyes and give out a loud, strained *tssh-schleek*. Despite his lack of musical talent, the male remains smug and proud, posing with his bill held high.

• In fall, large flocks of Common Grackles are found in rural areas. Smaller bands occasionally venture into urban neighborhoods, where they assert their dominance at backyard bird feeders.

Other ID: female is smaller, duller and browner than male. *Juvenile:* dull brown overall; dark eyes.
Size: L 11–13½ in; W 17 in.
Voice: song is a series of harsh, strained notes ending with a metallic squeak: *tssh-schleek* or *gri-de-leeek;* call is a quick, loud *swaaaack* or *chaack.*
Status: common permanent resident.
Habitat: wetlands, hedgerows, fields, riparian woodlands and along the edges of coniferous forests and woodlands; also shrubby parks and gardens.

Similar Birds

Rusty Blackbird

Brewer's Blackbird

European Starling
(p. 140)

long, keeled tail

long, heavy bill

yellow eyes

iridescent plumage often looks blackish

purple morph

Nesting: singly or in a small colony; in dense tree, shrub or emergent vegetation; often near water; female builds a bulky, open cup nest of twigs, grass, plant fibers and mud and lines it with fine grass or feathers; brown-blotched, pale blue eggs are 1⅛ x ⅞ in; female incubates 4–5 eggs for 12–14 days.

Did You Know?

At night, grackles commonly roost with groups of European Starlings, Red-winged Blackbirds and even Brown-headed Cowbirds.

Look For

The Common Grackle has a long, heavy bill and a lengthy, wedge-shaped tail that trails behind in flight.

Brown-headed Cowbird

Molothrus ater

These nomads historically followed bison herds across the Great Plains (they now follow cattle), so they never stayed in one area long enough to build and tend a nest. Instead, cowbirds lay their eggs in other birds' nests, relying on the unsuspecting adoptive parents to incubate the eggs and feed the aggressive young. Orioles, warblers, vireos and tanagers are among the most affected species. Increased livestock farming and fragmentation of forests has encouraged the expansion of the cowbird's range. It is known to parasitize more than 140 bird species.

Other ID: dark eyes; thick, conical bill.
Size: *L* 6–8 in; *W* 12 in.
Voice: song is a high, liquidy gurgle: *glug-ahl-whee* or *bubbloozeee;* call is a squeaky, high-pitched *seep, psee* or *wee-tse-tse* or fast, chipping *ch-ch-ch-ch-ch-ch.*
Status: common permanent resident.
Habitat: agricultural and residential areas, usually fields, woodland edges, roadsides, landfills and areas near cattle.

Similar Birds

Rusty Blackbird

Brewer's Blackbird

Red-winged Blackbird
(p. 168)

pale throat

dark brown head

light brown underparts with faint streaking

iridescent, green-blue body plumage looks glossy black

short, squared tail

Nesting: does not build a nest; female lays up to 40 eggs a year in the nests of other birds, usually 1 egg per nest; brown-speckled, whitish eggs are ⅞ x ⅝ in; eggs hatch after 10–13 days.

Did You Know?

When courting a female, the male cowbird points his bill upward to the sky, fans his tail and wings and utters a loud *squeek*.

Look For

When cowbirds feed in flocks, they hold their back ends up high, with their tails sticking straight up in the air.

Orchard Oriole
Icterus spurius

Orchards may once have been favored haunts of this oriole, but since orchards are now heavily sprayed and manicured, it is unlikely that you will ever see this bird in such a locale. Instead, the Orchard Oriole is most commonly found in large shade trees that line roads, paths and streams. Smaller than all other North American orioles, the Orchard Oriole is one of only two oriole species commonly found in the eastern United States. • These orioles are frequent victims of nest parasitism by Brown-headed Cowbirds. In some parts of its breeding range, over half of Orchard Oriole nests are parasitized by cowbirds.

Other ID: *Female* and *immature:* olive upperparts; yellow to olive yellow underparts.
Size: *L* 6–7 in; *W* 9½ in.
Voice: song is a loud, rapid, varied series of whistled notes; call is a quick *chuck*.
Status: fairly common summer resident.
Habitat: open woodlands, suburban parklands, forest edges, hedgerows and groves of shade trees.

Similar Birds

Baltimore Oriole

Summer Tanager

Scarlet Tanager
(p. 152)

dark wings with white wing bar and feather edgings

black "hood"

faint, white wingbars on dusky gray wings

♂ ♀

chestnut underparts, shoulder and rump

black tail

Nesting: in a fork of a deciduous tree or shrub; female builds a hanging pouch nest woven from grass and plant fibers; darkly blotched, pale bluish white eggs are ¾ x ⁹⁄₁₆ in; female incubates 4–5 eggs for about 12–15 days.

Did You Know?

The Orchard Oriole is one of the first species to migrate following breeding and is usually absent by the beginning of August.

Look For

These birds are best seen in spring when eager males hop from branch to branch, singing their quick and musical courtship songs.

House Finch
Carpodacus mexicanus

A native to western North America, the House Finch was brought to eastern parts of the continent as an illegally captured cage bird known as the "Hollywood Finch." In the early 1940s, New York pet shop owners released their birds to avoid prosecution and fines, and it is likely the descendants of those birds that have colonized our area. In fact, the House Finch is now commonly found throughout the continental U.S. and has been introduced in Hawaii. • Only the resourceful House Finch has been aggressive and stubborn enough to successfully outcompete the House Sparrow. Both birds flourish in urban environments.

Other ID: streaked undertail coverts. *Female:* indistinct facial patterning; heavily streaked underparts.
Size: *L* 5–6 in; *W* 9½ in.
Voice: song is a bright, disjointed warble lasting about 3 seconds, often ending with a harsh *jeeer* or *wheer;* flight call is a sweet *cheer,* given singly or in series.
Status: common permanent resident.
Habitat: cities, towns and agricultural areas.

Similar Birds

Purple Finch

House Sparrow
(p. 182)

short bill with
curved upperbill

bright red "eyebrow,"
forecrown, throat
and breast

brown-streaked
back

♂

♀

heavily
streaked flanks

square tail

Nesting: in a cavity, building, dense foliage or
abandoned bird nest; open cup nest is made of
grass and twigs; sparsely marked, pale blue eggs
are ¾ x ⁹/₁₆ in; female incubates 4–5 eggs for
12–14 days.

Did You Know?

The male House Finch's
plumage varies in color
from light yellow to bright
red, but females will
choose the reddest males
with which to breed.

Look For

In flight, the House Finch has
a square tail, whereas the
similar-looking Purple Finch
has a sharply notched tail.

American Goldfinch
Carduelis tristis

Like vibrant rays of sunshine, American Goldfinches cheerily flutter over weedy fields, gardens and along roadsides. It is hard to miss their jubilant *po-ta-to-chip* call and their distinctive, undulating flight style. • Because these acrobatic birds regularly feed while hanging upside down, finch feeders are designed with the seed-openings below the perches. These feeders discourage the more aggressive House Sparrows, which feed upright, from stealing the seeds. Use niger or black-oil sunflower seeds to attract American Goldfinches to your bird feeder.

Other ID: *Breeding male:* orange bill and legs.
Female: yellow throat and breast; yellow-green belly.
Nonbreeding male: olive brown back; yellow-tinged head; gray underparts.
Size: *L* 4½–5 in; *W* 9 in.
Voice: song is a long, varied series of trills, twitters, warbles and hissing notes; calls include *po-ta-to-chip* or *per-chic-or-ee* (often delivered in flight) and a whistled *dear-me, see-me*.
Status: common permanent resident.
Habitat: weedy fields, woodland edges, meadows, riparian areas, parks and gardens.

Similar Birds

Evening Grosbeak   Wilson's Warbler

yellow-green
upperparts

black cap extends
onto forehead

♀

black wings and tail
with white wing bars

white rump and
undertail coverts

breeding

♂

Nesting: in a fork of a deciduous tree; compact cup nest is made of plant fibers, grass and spider silk; pale bluish, spotted eggs are ⅝ x ½ in; female incubates 4–6 eggs for 12–14 days.

Did You Know?

These birds nest in late summer to ensure that there is a dependable source of seeds from thistles and dandelions to feed their young.

Look For

American Goldfinches delight in perching on late-summer thistle heads or poking through dandelion patches in search of seeds.

House Sparrow
Passer domesticus

A black "mask" and "bib" adorn the male of this adaptive, aggressive species. The House Sparrow's tendency to usurp territory has led to a decline in native bird populations. This sparrow will even help itself to the convenience of another bird's home, such as a bluebird or Cliff Swallow nest or a Purple Martin house. • This abundant and conspicuous bird was introduced to North America in the 1850s as part of a plan to control the insects that were damaging grain and cereal crops. As it turns out, these birds are largely vegetarian!

Other ID: *Breeding male:* gray crown; black bill; dark, mottled upperparts; gray underparts; white wing bar. *Female:* indistinct facial pattern; plain gray-brown overall; streaked upperparts.
Size: L 5½–6½ in; W 9½ in.
Voice: song is a plain, familiar *cheep-cheep-cheep-cheep;* call is a short *chill-up.*
Status: common to locally abundant permanent resident.
Habitat: townsites, urban and suburban areas, farmyards and agricultural areas, railroad yards and other developed areas.

Similar Birds

House Finch (p. 178)

Look For

In spring, House Sparrows feast on the buds of fruit trees and will sometimes eat lettuce from backyard gardens.

buffy "eyebrow"

light gray "cheek"

chestnut nape

♀

♂

black lores and "bib"

grayish, unstreaked underparts

Nesting: often communal; in a human-made structure, ornamental shrub or natural cavity; pair builds a large dome nest of grass, twigs and plant fibers; gray-speckled, white to greenish eggs are ⅞ x ⅝ in; pair incubates 4–6 eggs for 10–13 days.

Did You Know?

House Sparrows have a high reproductive output. A pair may raise up to four clutches per year, with up to eight young per clutch.

Glossary

accipiter: a forest hawk (genus *Accipiter*); characterized by a long tail and short, rounded wings; feeds mostly on birds.

brood: *n.* a family of young from one hatching; *v.* to sit on eggs so as to hatch them.

buteo: a high-soaring hawk (genus *Buteo*); characterized by broad wings and short, wide tails; feeds mostly on small mammals and other land animals.

cere: a fleshy area at the base of a bird's bill that contains the nostrils.

clutch: the number of eggs laid by the female at one time.

corvid: a member of the crow family (Corvidae); includes crows, jays, ravens and magpies.

covey: a group of birds, usually grouse or quail.

crop: an enlargement of the esophagus; serves as a storage structure and (in pigeons) has glands that produce secretions.

dabbling: a foraging technique used by ducks, in which the head and neck are submerged but the body and tail remain on the water's surface; dabbling ducks can usually walk easily on land, can take off without running and have brightly colored speculums.

eclipse plumage: a cryptic plumage, similar to that of females, worn by some male ducks in autumn when they molt their flight feathers and consequently are unable to fly.

fledgling: a young bird that has left the nest but is dependent upon its parents.

flushing: a behavior in which frightened birds explode into flight in response to a disturbance.

flycatching: a feeding behavior in which the bird leaves a perch, snatches an insect in midair and returns to the same perch.

hawking: attempting to catch insects through aerial pursuit.

irruptive: when a bird is abundant in some years and almost absent in others.

leading edge: the front edge of the wing as viewed from below.

mantle: feathers of the back and upperside of folded wings.

morph: one of several alternate plumages displayed by members of a species.

niche: an ecological role filled by a species.

nocturnal: active during the night.

polyandry: a mating strategy in which one female breeds with several males.

precocial: a bird that is relatively well developed at hatching; precocial birds usually have open eyes, extensive down and are fairly mobile.

primaries: the outermost flight feathers.

raptor: a carnivorous (meat-eating) bird; includes eagles, hawks, falcons and owls.

riparian: refers to habitat along riverbanks.

rufous: rusty red in color.

sexual dimorphism: a difference in plumage, size, or other characteristics between males and females of the same species.

speculum: a brightly colored patch on the wings of many dabbling ducks.

stoop: a steep dive through the air, usually performed by birds of prey while foraging or during courtship displays.

Checklist

The following checklist contains 369 species of birds that have been officially recorded in Kentucky. Species are grouped by family and listed in taxonomic order in accordance with the *A.O.U. Check-list of North American Birds* (7th ed.) and its supplements. The following risk categories as identified by the Kentucky Department of Fish and Wildlife Resources are also noted: extinct or extirpated (ex), endangered (en), threatened (th) and special concern (sc).

We wish to thank the Kentucky Ornithological Society for providing the information for this checklist.

Waterfowl
❏ Greater White-fronted Goose
❏ Snow Goose
❏ Ross's Goose
❏ Cackling Goose
❏ Canada Goose
❏ Brant
❏ Mute Swan
❏ Trumpeter Swan (ex)
❏ Tundra Swan
❏ Wood Duck
❏ Gadwall
❏ Eurasian Wigeon
❏ American Wigeon
❏ American Black Duck
❏ Mallard
❏ Blue-winged Teal (th)
❏ Cinnamon Teal
❏ Northern Shoveler (en)
❏ Northern Pintail
❏ Green-winged Teal
❏ Canvasback
❏ Redhead
❏ Ring-necked Duck
❏ Tufted Duck
❏ Greater Scaup
❏ Lesser Scaup
❏ King Eider
❏ Harlequin Duck
❏ Surf Scoter
❏ White-winged Scoter
❏ Black Scoter
❏ Long-tailed Duck
❏ Bufflehead
❏ Common Goldeneye
❏ Hooded Merganser (th)
❏ Common Merganser

❏ Red-breasted Merganser
❏ Masked Duck
❏ Ruddy Duck

Grouse & Allies
❏ Ruffed Grouse
❏ Greater Prairie-Chicken (ex)
❏ Wild Turkey

New World Quail
❏ Northern Bobwhite

Loons
❏ Red-throated Loon
❏ Pacific Loon
❏ Common Loon
❏ Yellow-billed Loon

Grebes
❏ Pied-billed Grebe (en)
❏ Horned Grebe
❏ Red-necked Grebe
❏ Eared Grebe
❏ Western Grebe

Petrels
❏ Black-capped Petrel

Storm-Petrels
❏ Band-rumped Storm-Petrel

Gannets
❏ Northern Gannet

Pelicans
❏ American White Pelican
❏ Brown Pelican

Cormorants
❏ Double-crested Cormorant (en)

Darters
❑ Anhinga (ex)

Herons
❑ American Bittern
❑ Least Bittern (th)
❑ Great Blue Heron (sc)
❑ Great Egret (en)
❑ Snowy Egret
❑ Little Blue Heron (en)
❑ Tricolored Heron
❑ Reddish Egret
❑ Cattle Egret (sc)
❑ Green Heron
❑ Black-crowned Night-Heron (th)
❑ Yellow-crowned Night-Heron (th)

Ibises
❑ White Ibis
❑ Glossy Ibis
❑ White-faced Ibis
❑ Roseate Spoonbill

Storks
❑ Wood Stork

Vultures
❑ Black Vulture
❑ Turkey Vulture

Kites, Hawks & Eagles
❑ Osprey (th)
❑ Swallow-tailed Kite (ex)
❑ White-tailed Kite
❑ Mississippi Kite (sc)
❑ Bald Eagle (th)
❑ Northern Harrier (th)
❑ Sharp-shinned Hawk (sc)
❑ Cooper's Hawk
❑ Northern Goshawk
❑ Red-shouldered Hawk
❑ Broad-winged Hawk
❑ Red-tailed Hawk
❑ Rough-legged Hawk
❑ Golden Eagle

Falcons
❑ American Kestrel
❑ Merlin
❑ Peregrine Falcon (en)
❑ Prairie Falcon

Rails, Gallinules & Coots
❑ Yellow Rail
❑ King Rail (en)
❑ Virginia Rail
❑ Sora
❑ Purple Gallinule
❑ Common Moorhen (th)
❑ American Coot (en)

Cranes
❑ Sandhill Crane
❑ Whooping Crane (ex)

Plovers
❑ Black-bellied Plover
❑ American Golden-Plover
❑ Semipalmated Plover
❑ Piping Plover
❑ Killdeer

Stilts & Avocets
❑ Black-necked Stilt
❑ American Avocet

Sandpipers & Allies
❑ Greater Yellowlegs
❑ Lesser Yellowlegs
❑ Solitary Sandpiper
❑ Willet
❑ Spotted Sandpiper (en)
❑ Upland Sandpiper
❑ Whimbrel
❑ Hudsonian Godwit
❑ Marbled Godwit
❑ Ruddy Turnstone
❑ Red Knot
❑ Sanderling
❑ Semipalmated Sandpiper
❑ Western Sandpiper
❑ Least Sandpiper
❑ White-rumped Sandpiper
❑ Baird's Sandpiper
❑ Pectoral Sandpiper
❑ Dunlin
❑ Curlew Sandpiper
❑ Stilt Sandpiper
❑ Buff-breasted Sandpiper
❑ Ruff
❑ Short-billed Dowitcher
❑ Long-billed Dowitcher
❑ Wilson's Snipe
❑ American Woodcock
❑ Wilson's Phalarope
❑ Red-necked Phalarope
❑ Red Phalarope

Gulls & Allies
❑ Pomarine Jaeger
❑ Long-tailed Jaeger
❑ Laughing Gull
❑ Franklin's Gull

❏ Little Gull
❏ Black-headed Gull
❏ Bonaparte's Gull
❏ Ring-billed Gull
❏ California Gull
❏ Herring Gull
❏ Thayer's Gull
❏ Iceland Gull
❏ Lesser Black-backed Gull
❏ Glaucous Gull
❏ Great Black-backed Gull
❏ Sabine's Gull
❏ Black-legged Kittiwake
❏ Gull-billed Tern
❏ Caspian Tern
❏ Common Tern
❏ Forster's Tern
❏ Least Tern (en)
❏ Sooty Tern
❏ Black Tern (ex)
❏ Long-billed Murrelet

Pigeons & Doves
❏ Rock Pigeon
❏ Band-tailed Pigeon
❏ Eurasian Collared-Dove
❏ White-winged Dove
❏ Mourning Dove
❏ Passenger Pigeon (ex)
❏ Inca Dove
❏ Common Ground-Dove

Parrots
❏ Carolina Parakeet (ex)

Cuckoos
❏ Black-billed Cuckoo
❏ Yellow-billed Cuckoo

Anis
❏ Groove-billed Ani

Barn Owls
❏ Barn Owl (sc)

Owls
❏ Eastern Screech-Owl
❏ Great Horned Owl
❏ Snowy Owl
❏ Barred Owl
❏ Long-eared Owl (en)
❏ Short-eared Owl (en)
❏ Northern Saw-whet Owl

Nightjars
❏ Common Nighthawk
❏ Chuck-will's-widow

❏ Whip-poor-will

Swifts
❏ Chimney Swift

Hummingbirds
❏ Green Violet-ear
❏ Ruby-throated Hummingbird
❏ Black-chinned Hummingbird
❏ Rufous Hummingbird

Kingfishers
❏ Belted Kingfisher

Woodpeckers
❏ Red-headed Woodpecker
❏ Red-bellied Woodpecker
❏ Yellow-bellied Sapsucker
❏ Downy Woodpecker
❏ Hairy Woodpecker
❏ Red-cockaded Woodpecker (ex)
❏ Northern Flicker
❏ Pileated Woodpecker
❏ Ivory-billed Woodpecker (ex)

Flycatchers
❏ Olive-sided Flycatcher
❏ Eastern Wood-Pewee
❏ Yellow-bellied Flycatcher
❏ Acadian Flycatcher
❏ Alder Flycatcher
❏ Willow Flycatcher
❏ Least Flycatcher (en)
❏ Eastern Phoebe
❏ Say's Phoebe
❏ Vermilion Flycatcher
❏ Ash-throated Flycatcher
❏ Great Crested Flycatcher
❏ Western Kingbird
❏ Eastern Kingbird
❏ Scissor-tailed Flycatcher

Shrikes
❏ Loggerhead Shrike
❏ Northern Shrike

Vireos
❏ White-eyed Vireo
❏ Bell's Vireo (sc)
❏ Yellow-throated Vireo
❏ Blue-headed Vireo
❏ Warbling Vireo
❏ Philadelphia Vireo
❏ Red-eyed Vireo

Jays & Crows
❏ Blue Jay

❏ American Crow
❏ Fish Crow (sc)
❏ Common Raven (th)

Larks
❏ Horned Lark

Swallows
❏ Purple Martin
❏ Tree Swallow
❏ Northern Rough-winged Swallow
❏ Bank Swallow (sc)
❏ Cliff Swallow
❏ Barn Swallow

Chickadees & Titmice
❏ Carolina Chickadee
❏ Black-capped Chickadee
❏ Tufted Titmouse

Nuthatches
❏ Red-breasted Nuthatch (en)
❏ White-breasted Nuthatch
❏ Brown-headed Nuthatch

Creepers
❏ Brown Creeper (en)

Wrens
❏ Rock Wren
❏ Carolina Wren
❏ Bewick's Wren (sc)
❏ House Wren
❏ Winter Wren
❏ Sedge Wren (sc)
❏ Marsh Wren

Kinglets
❏ Golden-crowned Kinglet
❏ Ruby-crowned Kinglet

Gnatcatchers
❏ Blue-gray Gnatcatcher

Thrushes
❏ Eastern Bluebird
❏ Mountain Bluebird
❏ Veery
❏ Gray-cheeked Thrush
❏ Swainson's Thrush
❏ Hermit Thrush
❏ Wood Thrush
❏ American Robin
❏ Varied Thrush

Mockingbirds & Thrashers
❏ Gray Catbird
❏ Northern Mockingbird
❏ Brown Thrasher

Starlings
❏ European Starling

Wagtails & Pipits
❏ American Pipit

Waxwings
❏ Cedar Waxwing

Wood-Warblers
❏ Bachman's Warbler (ex)
❏ Blue-winged Warbler
❏ Golden-winged Warbler (th)
❏ Tennessee Warbler
❏ Orange-crowned Warbler
❏ Nashville Warbler
❏ Northern Parula
❏ Yellow Warbler
❏ Chestnut-sided Warbler
❏ Magnolia Warbler
❏ Cape May Warbler
❏ Black-throated Blue Warbler
❏ Yellow-rumped Warbler
❏ Black-throated Gray Warbler
❏ Black-throated Green Warbler
❏ Blackburnian Warbler (th)
❏ Yellow-throated Warbler
❏ Pine Warbler
❏ Prairie Warbler
❏ Palm Warbler
❏ Bay-breasted Warbler
❏ Blackpoll Warbler
❏ Cerulean Warbler
❏ Black-and-white Warbler
❏ American Redstart
❏ Prothonotary Warbler
❏ Worm-eating Warbler
❏ Swainson's Warbler
❏ Ovenbird
❏ Northern Waterthrush
❏ Louisiana Waterthrush
❏ Kentucky Warbler
❏ Connecticut Warbler
❏ Mourning Warbler
❏ Common Yellowthroat
❏ Hooded Warbler
❏ Wilson's Warbler
❏ Canada Warbler (sc)
❏ Yellow-breasted Chat

Tanagers
❏ Summer Tanager
❏ Scarlet Tanager

Sparrows & Allies
❏ Green-tailed Towhee

❏ Spotted Towhee
❏ Eastern Towhee
❏ Bachman's Sparrow (en)
❏ American Tree Sparrow
❏ Chipping Sparrow
❏ Clay-colored Sparrow
❏ Field Sparrow
❏ Vesper Sparrow (en)
❏ Lark Sparrow (th)
❏ Savannah Sparrow (sc)
❏ Grasshopper Sparrow
❏ Henslow's Sparrow (sc)
❏ Le Conte's Sparrow
❏ Nelson's Sharp-tailed Sparrow
❏ Fox Sparrow
❏ Song Sparrow
❏ Lincoln's Sparrow
❏ Swamp Sparrow
❏ White-throated Sparrow
❏ Harris's Sparrow
❏ White-crowned Sparrow
❏ Dark-eyed Junco (sc)
❏ Lapland Longspur
❏ Smith's Longspur
❏ Snow Bunting

Grosbeaks & Buntings
❏ Northern Cardinal
❏ Rose-breasted Grosbeak (sc)
❏ Black-headed Grosbeak
❏ Blue Grosbeak

❏ Indigo Bunting
❏ Painted Bunting
❏ Dickcissel

Blackbirds & Allies
❏ Bobolink (sc)
❏ Red-winged Blackbird
❏ Eastern Meadowlark
❏ Western Meadowlark
❏ Yellow-headed Blackbird
❏ Rusty Blackbird
❏ Brewer's Blackbird
❏ Common Grackle
❏ Brown-headed Cowbird
❏ Orchard Oriole
❏ Bullock's Oriole
❏ Baltimore Oriole

Finches
❏ Purple Finch
❏ House Finch
❏ Red Crossbill
❏ White-winged Crossbill
❏ Common Redpoll
❏ Pine Siskin
❏ Lesser Goldfinch
❏ American Goldfinch
❏ Evening Grosbeak

Old World Sparrows
❏ House Sparrow
❏ Eurasian Tree Sparrow

Select References

American Ornithologists' Union. 1998. *Check-list of North American Birds*. 7th ed. (and its supplements). American Ornithologists' Union, Washington, DC.

Munroe, Burt L., Jr. 1994. *The Birds of Kentucky*. Indiana University Press, Bloomington, IN.

National Geographic Society. 2002. *Field Guide to the Birds of North America*. 4th ed. National Geographic Society, Washington, DC.

Palmer-Ball, Brainerd L., Jr. 1996. *The Kentucky Breeding Bird Atlas*. University Press of Kentucky, Lexington.

Peterson, Roger Tory. 2002. *Birds of Eastern and Central North America*. 5th ed. Houghton Mifflin, New York.

Roth, Sally. 1998. *Attracting Birds to Your Backyard*. Rodale Press, Emmaus, PA.

Sibley, D.A. 2000. *National Audubon Society: The Sibley Guide to Birds*. Alfred A. Knopf, New York.

Sibley, D.A. 2002. *Sibley's Birding Basics*. Alfred A. Knopf, New York.

Index